Gardening for the
Physically Handicapped and Elderly

Gardening for the Physically Handicapped and Elderly

MARY CHAPLIN
In association with the *Royal Horticultural Society*

Foreword by Lady Hamilton OBE, MA
Chairman of The Disabled Living Foundation

B.T. BATSFORD LTD, LONDON

To
The Members of the Gardening Club
at the Royal Hospital and Home for
Incurables, Putney

First published 1978
First paperback edition 1980
© Mary Chaplin, 1978

ISBN 0 7134 1082 5

Printed and bound in Great Britain by
Redwood-Burn Ltd, Trowbridge and Esher
for the publishers B.T. Batsford Ltd,
4 Fitzhardinge Street, London W1H 0AH

Contents

List of Line Drawings

List of Illustrations

Acknowledgments

I would like to express my appreciation to Mrs Kay Brooks, Senior Occupational Therapist, Mount Vernon Hospital, for her most helpful criticism of several chapters in this book. Also to Mr Peter Thoday, Senior Lecturer in Horticulture, University of Bath, for helpful discussions on the subject of this book.

I would also like to acknowledge photographs numbers 11, 12, 13, 14, 15 and 16 taken at the Disabled Living Foundation's demonstration gardens; numbers 1, 2, 6, 8, 20, 21, 22, 23 and 24 taken at the Royal Horticultural Society's Garden, Wisley, Surrey; number 9 Mrs M. Lorek, Director of the Greater London Association for the Disabled; number 18 Mrs M. Bigmore; and also the Royal Hospital and Home for Incurables.

Last but no means least I express my gratitude to all the physically handicapped people with whom I have worked in gardening, and who have taught me so much.

Eric Fairbairn and May Hall, cover picture

Foreword by
Lady Hamilton OBE, MA
Chairman, Disabled Living Foundation

Gardening is a much-loved activity of the British and comes second in popularity as a leisure pursuit to watching television. There isn't any reason for thinking that disabled people should be different from the rest of us about what they would like to do; only different in whether they can do it or not. Like the rest of us they may need help in starting or carrying on a leisure pursuit. In this country those who are experts in gardening for disabled people can be numbered on the fingers of one hand. Hence, unless the disabled person is fortunate in where he or she lives, it is difficult to get local advice and books, and the enquiry service of the Disabled Living Foundation may be the only available source of information.

The Information Bank of the D.L.F's enquiry service was built up and organized for many years by the author of this book, Miss Mary Chaplin, when she was D.L.F. Gardening Adviser. She is one of the few national authorities in a subject which has only recently been developed. Readers will find that she has written here an exceptionally helpful book dealing persuasively and imaginatively with the many problems which disability can bring to gardeners, whether they are beginners or would-be beginners of any age, never having gardened before, or keen and knowledgeable gardeners who have subsequently become disabled. Miss Chaplin knows most of these problems: she knows the pitfalls, the difficulties and the solutions. Here they are all carefully listed and presented as only a dedicated and learned horticulturalist can present them. Through her suggestions disabled people may be able to join more with other gardeners in what many think to be the happiest of all our national leisure pursuits.

1 Introduction

Gardening is an activity enjoyed by very many people, and amongst keen gardeners there are some who have a physical handicap and cannot always work in the conventional manner. Such handicaps have a very wide range; increasing age is one, the almost inevitable 'bad back' distresses many gardeners and curtails much of the work which needs doing. Then there are the more severely disabled, people who have become paralysed through a stroke or suffered serious injuries in a car accident. In the case of some of these categories, any work which is accomplished, is done by sheer will-power combined with great physical effort. Others long to be out-of-doors but are not sure what they can do when they get there. The range of physical limitations is wide and often help is needed whether the gardener is ambulant or wheelchair-bound. This book attempts to give ideas not only to the gardener who has a disability but also to relatives and friends who may be able to give a hand in re-organising the garden.

Many people overcome a handicap within the home because it has been adapted to their needs, but when it comes to the garden they are somewhat wary of venturing outside as there seem to be so many hazards. Similar confidence may be gained in the garden as in the home if the garden is designed with the disabled person's difficulty in view. The right tools will also make a great difference; these are discussed in chapter 2 and helpful tools suggested where applicable.

Not all gardening is out-of-doors however; propagation and growing house plants indoors is a challenge to anyone. A collection of these subjects can soon take over the house, with African violets in kitchen and bathroom; succulents and cacti in sunny windows, and various other plants spilling out from every odd corner, so that attention to these plants can be all-absorbing. This is the case in some bedrooms at the Royal Hospital and Home for Incurables at Putney, where under the greatest of physical handicaps, people living there grow good plants and also enjoy the meetings of the garden club they have formed.

Window-box gardening is another way of growing plants which can be tended from indoors, with plants for every season of the year, including dwarf vegetables and herbs. And a patio garden or balcony may be just the right size for the person who cannot or does not wish to move far. Either area can be arranged with plants in containers or small raised beds, so that everything is within reach.

Whatever the difficulty, if someone is a gardener at heart, ways and means must be found to continue this hobby, if only in a very small way; similarly those who have never thought of trying to grow plants, after reading this book it is hoped will see that there are more possibilities than they thought and it is hoped, will be encouraged to make an attempt themselves. The thought comes to mind of a badly paralysed person who could not use her fingers and whose only way of potting was to lift the plant between the backs of her hands, and drop it into the new pot. Yet the plants always seemed to grow well for her.

One difficulty is not physical, but the expense of putting ideas into practice. Where possible alternative ideas are given (e.g. for raised beds and containers) that do not cost too much in materials and labour. For financial reasons and because help may only be available spasmodically, it is suggested that a garden should be altered a little at a time; otherwise it might be too daunting, monetarily as well as physically, to start. After all a patch of nettles away from the house is a good breeding ground for many of our loveliest butterflies! Weeds sometimes have their uses! (Although, for situations where they are not welcome, there is included a chapter on weed control).

Finally and of great importance is the actual planting of the garden. Shrubs that grow tall and need pruning every year are of little use to the wheelchair gardener, or the person who has a very weak grip and cannot manage secateurs. Equally, low-growing plants are useless to the person who cannot bend and can only work in an upright standing position; for such people climbing plants on a fence or pergola are probably the easiest to manage. Some people in wheelchairs who are strong in the upper limbs, scorn easy plants and like the challenge of training cordon or espalier fruit trees; mowing the lawn; and even digging. The whole planning of the garden however hinges on the gardener's physical ability, bearing in mind whether that ability is likely to deteriorate or not. Naturally the ultimate choice of plants is personal, but with many plants to choose from the choice of the right ones can be a positive aid to the gardener, rather than causing him difficulty. When different plants are mentioned, the care needed for them is also given, so that the easiest plants may be chosen by those persons with the greatest difficulties.

When a garden is being laid out, if possible the handicapped person should follow the construction, giving his opinion throughout, for after all it is he who is going to work in it. If a garden is very small then the whole area could be paved, with a mixture of ground level and raised beds or containers; this can look most attractive. Possibly a corner would be suitable for the ground level bed, where a small-sized tree could be planted with low-growing shrubs. This bed would almost maintain itself and be a focal point to view from the house.

Raised beds and containers need to be 4 feet apart for easy movement and to allow turning space for a wheelchair. L or T shaped raised beds are more attractive than rectangular ones. Circular containers such as those made from a car wheel give a different shape, while troughs or sinks are admirable for dwarf conifers and rock plants. Should the area be large enough a raised pool is possible; this can be expensive to build, but a smaller and cheaper one may be made by using a raised bed of lorry tyres (see chapter 2) with a deep plastic bowl sunk in the top one, leaving a border of soil between bowl and tyre edge for planting. If the only area for a raised bed is in the shade, then a bed may be made of peat blocks. In the sun peat blocks eventually dry out and crumble.

When designing a small area it will look its best if it is uncluttered, and any trees, shrubs etc. need to be in the right proportion to the area. Too large a tree dwarfs a small garden while small raised beds or containers are more attractive than one large raised bed. It should also be remembered that plants are just as variable as human beings and if they are to give of their best, they need the right conditions; some like a peat soil, while others prefer lime, while the majority are happy in a fairly neutral soil.

The fence or wall around a small garden could be used for trained fruit trees. Where the garden is large enough and there is a greenhouse and shed these need to be as near the house as possible.

All the plants mentioned in the book have been checked as being available from nurserymen by mail order as many people are unable to visit a garden centre.

A complete book would be needed on the growing of plants in a greenhouse; here, general principles are given including automation.

Where a person has a large garden but only uses a paved area adjoining the house, the problem is 'what to do with the rest of the garden not in use?' If the gardener is severely handicapped he could possibly let a friend or neighbour cultivate this area as a vegetable plot with the possible advantage of receiving some fresh vegetables in return. Many people with deep-freezers are only too glad to have land extra to their own gardens.

There are some gardeners who excel in the growing of one particular kind of flower, such as irises, dahlias, gladioli or chrysanthemums and they often raise new varieties, but once again invariably their gardens are not large enough for these activities, especially when there is a great number of seedlings to be grown in the process of breeding plants. Such gardeners would be only too glad to have the use of more land, while the flowers they grow would be a bonus to the owner of the garden without the worry of cultivation.

For either of these projects the nearest allotment or horticultural society could be approached. This is possibly the easiest method of coping with the area of garden that is in excess of the gardener's needs.

The elderly or slightly handicapped person may, however, be loath to part with any part of the garden. The 'excess' area could then perhaps be made into a 'natural' garden with shrubs and ground-cover plants interspersed with bulbs which increase themselves. If this is decided upon, many of the shrubs and plants may be propagated by cuttings in a cold frame, particularly if there are any gardening friends who can spare come cuttings.

The above are but ideas, and the reader should not be deterred by thinking of the work involved. If a start is made in a small area near the house, and the gardener becomes engrossed, he will soon know what he does or does not want in his garden, then, with help from relatives or groups from outside, he can gradually develop further areas as and when he wishes.

For all elderly or handicapped gardeners there is a golden rule, and that is to start on one job and *before* feeling any tiredness stop or change to another then come back to the first one or possibly start a third. This idea will probably not be liked by the tidy minded, but it means that specific muscles are not taxed for too long and gardening can be continued over a greater period.

So, having decided gardening can be really worthwhile, remember the Chinese proverb: 'If you have two pennies spend one on a loaf and the other on a flower, the bread will give you life and the flower a reason for living.'

2 Adaptations and Innovations

Many people are ill-prepared for retirement, then, suddenly, it is upon them. The garden in which they had hoped to spend so much time seems too large, and the amount of work to be done in it more a burden than a pleasure. A major alteration which appears necessary causes either too much effort or proves too costly. Similarly, people who are handicapped through a disability feel that many things in the garden are just that bit beyond their control.

Ideally, the whole garden could be re-designed and laid out to suit individual needs. This is not always possible, but many small adjustments may be made a little at a time. It is only occasionally that people move into a new house with a bare plot to make into a garden. The greatest difficulty and the greatest challenge can lie in altering a garden which already exists.

For people who are severely handicapped a paved area with raised beds and/or plant containers is most suitable, particularly if the area is close to or adjoins the house. Such a patio need only to be small to start with, but so designed that it can be enlarged as and when needed. Various other areas in the garden may also be developed gradually for the handicapped person's use, and while this may take place progressively, increasing the area a little at a time, the rest of the garden also has to be considered. An untidy wilderness is different from a 'planned' wild garden, and later chapters will give ideas for planting such areas with a view to ease of maintenance as well as to give pleasure in the plants themselves and the birds and insects they attract.

For a handicapped person the major factor in the garden is that of getting around it. This sounds a simple matter, but when mobility is only possible with a walking frame, the aid of two sticks, or in a wheelchair, it can become most hazardous if conditions underfoot are bad. So, the first concentration must be on paths.

Handrails

For disabled but ambulant people and those who are elderly: a single handrail on one side of the path may be sufficient. The side on which the rail is placed will depend upon whether the person using it is right or left handed. If the rail should be alongside a border of shrubs or tall growing plants, it can be used as a light support, leaving one hand free for trimming and dead-heading etc. A handrail is also useful for going up or down steps. Sometimes a double handrail i.e. one either side is needed. A handrail can even be essential for only one step.

Materials for constructing a handrail can vary. Wood is the most attractive but galvanised piping may be better for the person concerned, as the hand can slip along it more easily. Sometimes a visit to a scrap-yard is worthwhile and material suitable for constructing handrails can be obtained at bargain prices. Whatever material is used, the uprights need to be absolutely firm, and the horizontal rail attached so that there is not the slightest play or movement, otherwise it defeats its object. It is not advisable to grow any plants up the supports, as such plants would need attention. Odd growths sticking out could easily trip a person using the rail, and no plant growth should encumber the rail.

Useful as a handrail can be as a help in mobility it is of little use if the paths are rough and uneven, or the surface is slippery, especially after rainfall. Such paths are dangerous for anyone walking with the aid of sticks or using a wheelchair. Statistics show that the majority of accidents occur in the home and garden, so good safe garden paths are essential for everyone.

17

Paths

There are three main considerations in making a new path or
renovating an old one, viz, safety, aesthetic appeal and cost.
Safety naturally takes priority and this includes a level surface made of non-slip material and of sufficient width for any
aid a disabled person might use such as a walking frame or
wheelchair. The aesthetic appeal is personal. Paving slabs
are the most attractive, but they are expensive and both concrete and tarmacadam are also used; the latter mainly where
the garden is in a public park or hospital rehabilitation unit.
Weeds, and suckers of certain plants and trees e.g. Japanese
knotweed and poplar, will push their way through tarmac
and distrupt it, thus making it unsafe. Concrete has a grey
numb colour, but colourants are obtainable which may be
used to render it more attractive. One of these colourants is
offered (in small quantities if desired) by Shell Composites
Ltd; the colouring is permanent and unaffected by sunlight.
The smallest quantity available is 250 grams (approx. 8 oz)
and full instructions for use are given.

It is unsafe to discuss the cost of making a path with con-
stantly rising prices, but when some free labour can be
enlisted from a voluntary organisation or from friends and
relations, the cost is only for the materials.

Concrete, once favoured as being reasonably cheap, has
now become more expensive, with rather heavy work
involved in the mixing and laying. If helpers are available,
and willing to tackle a concrete path, a D.I.Y. shop often has
a concrete mixer for hire. Shuttering is necessary as a
'mould' to shape the path, to form square edges, and to enable a level surface to be tamped into position while the mix is
wet. A thickness of 3 in. over a well-rammed hardcore of
brick rubble is desirable. Recommended proportions for concrete suitable for a durable path are 1 part of volume cement,
5 parts ¾ in. ballast and approximately ¾ part water. Care
must be taken not to make the mixture too wet and sloppy
otherwise a dusty path will result. Some people prefer
ready-mixed concrete while others use a proprietory mixture
of aggregate and cement ready for mixing with water. A
non-slip surface can be made by tamping the wet concrete in

to slight ridges or by brushing the surface with a stiff broom just before it sets. A swirling pattern can be left if desired.

Full details for using cement can be found in a booklet entitled *Concrete in Garden-making* by Nicolette Franck published by the Cement and Concrete Association, 52 Grosvenor Gardens, London SW1W OAQ. At the time of writing (1977) this is free on request and is a most useful book.

The width of the path depends upon the width of the wheelchair for which it is to be used. A minimum width of 3 feet with 4 feet for turning is essential. Path makers often forget that wheelchairs must return! A width of 3 feet is also comfortable for anyone using two sticks or when the assistance of another person walking alongside is needed. The path should preferably curve gently without sharp turns.

Paving slabs vary widely in size, colour, pattern of surface and cost; the majority are non-slip, but this should always be checked before buying. When choosing slabs, it is advisable (if possible) for anyone with a mobility difficulty to try their feet over the various surfaces available to check suitability. Some makes, e.g. Perfecta Paving Marshalite, whilst being non-slip, allow the feet to glide over very easily while others have a 'pimpled' or slightly roughened surface offering more resistance; this may be preferred. Slabs are available in a variety of colours offering considerable choice. Sizes range from 9 in. square upwards. Smaller sizes are suitable for smaller gardens. An important point to remember is that paving slabs when large are heavy to lift and place in position and that if the person doing the work is elderly or very young it can be very tiring. On the other hand an elderly woman has been observed laying a path of 9 in. square slabs without becoming too fatigued.

Paving slabs must not only be laid so that they are perfectly level, they must *remain* level and certainly not 'rock'. For this a cement mixture is best for laying them on. First the topsoil must be removed leaving a firm base, over which is raked sand or other fine material such as ashes. At this stage levels should be checked, using a straight edge and spirit level. The actual 'mix' that the slabs are laid on can vary slightly. One method is to lay the paving on to a dry mixture of 1 part cement and 3 parts sand (by volume). Rain and soil moisture will settle them firmly. If the weather is very dry, watering over with a fine-rosed watering can will have the same effect. Be careful to avoid drenching. Alternatively, the same mixture of sand and cement can be used with water added. If this method is used, either the wet mixture may be laid down and the slabs bedded on it, or less expensively, a dab of the wet mixture placed in the centre and at each corner of the slab which is firmly pressed into position using a straight-edge to make sure of the level. A slab with an edge sticking up only slightly can cause a person to trip and fall.

Paving slabs are laid with ¼ in. space between them, if a lathe of this thickness is used on its side between the slabs as they are laid, perfect symmetry will be obtained.

Tarmacadam, if used is best supplied and laid by specialist contractors.

Beds and Borders

These can be either at ground level or raised, depending upon the need of the user. Some people prefer gardening at ground level using long-handled tools, others prefer working in a standing or sitting position at a raised bed.

Ground-level beds

While existing paths may be quite adequate for the gardener's needs, the borders may cause difficulty because they are too wide. True, a wide bed or border is usually more attractive than a narrow one, but that is of little use if it has to be left uncared for by reason of difficulty of access. Bare soil is not safe to walk on as it is too uneven neither will it support a stick.

There are several ways of overcoming the difficulty. One is to make the border narrower with a firm path from which to work on both sides. Where access to the border is only practicable from one side its width should be limited to about 2 feet.

Another helpful measure which is simpler than narrowing the border is to provide stepping stones through the bed leading to firm paving slabs of at least 2 feet by 2 feet in size from which to stand and work. Circular paving slabs, to be seen at most garden centres, make attractive stepping stones through a border. They need to be placed fairly near together to suit the normal pace of the person concerned. They also need to be embedded firmly and to be perfectly level. A large paving slab, or two together can be placed every so often; i.e. where shrubs or roses need pruning, and all other plants within convenient reach can be tended from such vantage points. Stepping stones are not, however, suitable for people using any type of walking aid, as they are not really wide enough to take one. A stick going in to soft soil alongside the stepping stone would be hazardous.

For gardening at ground level the correct choice of tools is of greatest importance. There are many long-handled tools on the market, provided the person concerned has sufficient strength in the arms to use them.

Some such tools are extremely light in weight such as the Bestwaye weeder which resembles a very small rake mounted on a lightweight tubular metal handle 5 feet in length, the

Using the 'Bestwaye' weeder from a wheelchair

21

weeds being dragged out by the rake-like head. Wilkinsons offer two long-handled weed forks with flat tines, one of medium length and the other with a cranked handle 4 ft 8 in. long. They also offer a long-handled Dutch hoe and their Swoe; the latter, however, requires perfect control by the user otherwise plants as well as weeds are easily cut off! Another long-handled device is the Baronet Cut-and-Hold Flower Gatherer. This can be operated with one hand; it is 30 in. in length and with the additional length of the gardener's arm will enable dead flower heads quite a distance away to be removed. The cutting part of this tool has teeth which keep the flower or dead-head until it is brought close to the operator when it is released into a container. Long-handled pruners are heavier and therefore more difficult to use on anything at a distance, unless the gardener has very strong arms. With both narrow borders and long-handled tools, it is possible for people in wheelchairs to garden successfully at ground level, provided their upper limbs are flexible and strong.

Raised Beds

It is not always necessary to build raised beds unless the site happens to be quite flat. Advantage can be taken of a natural bank, or any difference in ground level made during levelling operations when house building.

Plants can be grown naturally in such a bank or it can be retained by a vertical wall of dry stone with plants growing in the interstices between the stones. Such banks and beds will need to be 'tailored' to suit the limitations of the gardener, taking into consideration whether a standing or sitting position is preferred for working. If the bank is no more than 2 feet in height it may be possible to have a border along the top of it. Flat pieces of stone placed at intervals will allow the gardener to sit and work to right and left in comparative comfort.

Terraced gardens also provide natural raised borders if the work is done from the lower levels; this is only possible where paths have been adapted with ramps for wheelchairs or with steps and handrails. Another feature seen in many gardens is two walls, 18 ins thick to two feet apart with soil in between. These can be of various heights or thicknesses to suit the convenience of the gardener or the plants to be grown. If the space occupied by soil is sufficiently wide it gives scope for growing quite a range of dwarf growing shrubs or a low hedge which can be tended from a sitting position.

If the garden is quite flat, then raised beds may be built for those who can only do gardening this way. Provided a person can walk without any kind of assistance a raised bed on grass is not out of the question, but the grass will need to be kept short right up to the base of the raised bed, and this could create a problem.

For a wheelchair, or where there is walking difficulty, the only answer is a firm non-slip surface around any raised bed such as paving or concrete; this needs to extend to 4 feet from the walls of the bed for easy unhampered movement. Much paving can give a hard appearance to a garden, particularly where the garden is small and there is not much room for natural growth, but suggestions for overcoming this will be dealt with in the chapter on plants and planting.

Raised beds can be made from various materials, such as walling stone, bricks, natural stone, large paving slabs, precast walling, peat blocks, and used motor tyres of various sizes. Natural stone is the most expensive, both as a material and for the labour needed in building, unless such stone happens to be quarried locally. Large paving stones 2 feet by 3 feet (up-ended) are widely used in hospital gardens and rehabilitation units. They are utilitarian and serve a good purpose; besides being very heavy to manipulate, they are not attractive in a garden.

Pre-cast walling (Banbury) needs the minimum of labour for assembly, but has to be in definite units. Beds made of this walling are useful for vegetable growing.

Used tyres are the least expensive of all. The only cost is for transport and some paint and a brush, and if care is taken in building they can look most attractive, especially when constructed of tyres of varying sizes. A further advantage is that of easy disposal if the bed is no longer required. One of the greatest difficulties is that of making brick or stone beds look really attractive because of the necessary size limitations. If accessible from both sides, the bed should not be more than 4 feet in width, which will allow the worker to reach to the centre of the bed without undue strain. If accessible from one side only the width must not exceed 2 feet. The optimum height of a raised bed to be used by a person seated in a wheelchair is 2 feet.

A pleasing effect can be obtained by arranging raised beds in geometrical patterns such as L's, T's or diamonds. For vegetables a fairly long straight bed is the most practical, though if too long a great deal of fatigue can be caused in going from side to side when working. Inevitably size will depend upon the ability of the gardener, and it will be advisable to experiment with a small raised bed at first to find out what can be managed.

The choice of materials for construction and the shape of the raised bed will depend, to some extent, on the person building it. For instance, if a wife wishes to make a raised bed for her husband who is a keen gardener but has suffered a stroke, she obviously could not manipulate heavy paving slabs such as are used in hospital gardens. She could, however, build a raised bed of peat blocks, or acquire some terra-cotta chimney pots (particularly the broad-topped ones from Victorian and Edwardian houses) and put them into place for him. There are instances where the gardener is suffering from a type of disablement which will not allow him to work from a sitting position and he can only work standing erect. In such cases the raised beds will need to be constructed to meet individual requirements and allow work to be done with as much comfort and convenience as possible.

Method of Building Once the site has been chosen for the raised bed, the surroundings are best paved, leaving natural soil beneath where the bed is to stand to allow for drainage. If bricks, block-walling, etc., is being used then footings are required in the same way as in building a house and foundations of concrete on a good base of hardcore are necessary. Be careful to establish a proper level with a spirit level. Should the bed be longer than 4 feet buttresses should be keyed into the walls on the inside of the bed at 4 foot intervals to give the necessary strength for supporting the weight of soil, especially when the soil is wet. This is

Attractive shapes for raised beds

absolutely *essential*.

Should the raised bed be built on a patio or existing pavement then 'weep-holes' at the base of the bed are needed for drainage. Circular beds are possible, but the diameter must not be greater than 4 foot which can restrict the design.

Beds made from peat blocks have a very attractive surface, and are naturally suitable for growing dwarf rhododendrons, dwarf azaleas and heathers, etc. Peat beds must be sited in partial shade and not exposed to continuous sunshine, otherwise the peat blocks will flake and gradually disintegrate. Spraying over with water can mitigate this, but it is a labour which should be avoided. Many gardens have shaded sites (possibly near to the house) which are normally difficult to utilise, and this would prove to be an ideal position for a peat bed.

Peat blocks are attractive and easy to handle. They usually arrive in plastic sacks and need a thorough soaking in water for at least 24 hours, longer if possible, before using. This can be done by either immersing the blocks in a tank of water, adding more water as it is soaked up by the blocks, or if the plastic sacks are not punctured during transit these can be filled with water before removing the blocks. When the peat blocks are removed from the sacks some may be found to be markedly curved in shape. If these are separated and placed on one side they may be used when building the bed to form a curve which will make the bed appear less formal and more pleasing to the eye. A shallow trench is taken out the width of a peat block defining the shape of the bed; the first layer of peat blocks is then set in this allowing the blocks to project one inch above soil level. As successive layers of blocks are added, soil must be rammed *very* firmly down at the back of each layer *as the work proceeds*. As the wall of the bed grows higher, there must be a slight batter inwards. There is one difficulty which may occur with wheelchairs. People not used to controlling their wheelchair may knock the peat wall with the bumpers; if this occurs often, it can gradually flake away the peat. This can be overcome by building a cement wall for the first 9 in. then continuing with the peat blocks. The plants put in the lowest level of the peat could then hang down and hide the cement.

The soil in the raised bed would depend upon what is to be grown in it. If it is to be the ordinary run of perennials, bulbs, bedding plants etc., garden soil can be used with the possible addition of some sand and peat especially if the soil tends to be heavy and of a clay-like consistency. If, on the other hand, it is to be used for ericaceous plants such as heathers and azaleas, a non-lime mixture will be needed. Such a planting can prove most interesting and rewarding. A raised bed of peat blocks as described above, planted with choice and unusual plants, could prove to be an achievement within the capacity of most gardeners including those not capable of the more arduous work of building with the more conventional building materials.

Raised beds made from old motor or lorry tyres sound somewhat sordid, and the picture of a car breaker's yard with its smell of oil and weeds growing about the place comes to mind. A tyre bed need not be like this, for with a little ingenuity and the right kind of planting, very attractive beds can be made. There is no limitation to either size or height and beds can be made to suit children or adults whether ambulant or in a wheelchair. Such beds can be constructed on a patio or even in a small back yard, and when suitably planted can transform dull and depressing surroundings into a place of beauty and cheerfulness as well as providing daily interest to the gardener. Lorry and coach tyres give a reasonable area for planting, depending upon what a person can manage. Except for a very young child, mini car tyres are too small; at the other extreme tractor tyres are too large as the centre cannot be reached, 4 feet overall diameter should be the maximum size. Lorry and the larger size car tyres are ideal. Car tyres can usually be obtained free of charge, but lorry and coach tyres may cost a little. First paint the tyres with emulsion paint. Do not use white as this is somewhat stark, rather choose a cream shade or pale pastel colour such as 'magnolia' or 'camellia'. Most plants and flowers tone in with these more natural shades. The secret of success in constructing tyre beds is the arrangement of the plants in relation to the tyres. Plants such as ivies in variety and other trailing hardy evergreens, including ferns if the

27

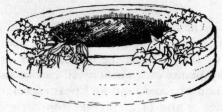

Methods of making and planting a raised bed from tyres

position is sunless, may be used and these should be planted as the bed is being built; they will look attractive even in winter. A column of tyres can consist of two, three or four. Two or three of these columns can form a crescent, the middle columns being higher than those on either side.

Tyres can be placed directly on to the hard surface of a paved area if desired, in which case rubble or stones for drainage are placed in the tyre to a depth of 4 in., over which is put a layer of coarse peat, or a piece of hessian sacking. The first layer of tyres is then filled with soil, packed well into the tyre walls and well firmed. Plants are then distributed round the outer tyre edges with the growing shoots facing outwards, after which the second layer of tyres is placed in position and the same procedure repeated until the desired height is reached. At this stage the whole centre of the tyre is planted. This type of raised bed can be added to or discarded as wished. It can be used for growing flowers, vegetables, or even strawberries in the sides of the bed. Details of planting are given in chapter 6.

For those confined to a wheelchair with very little ability to move or use their hands, a chimney pot is challenge enough. The tops vary in size, but most will take an upright pelargonium (geranium) with two ivy-leaved ones trailing down the side.

Occasionally wooden half-barrels may be obtained such as those used for pulp in the soft drinks industry. They should be treated with green Cuprinol wood preservative (which is harmless to plants). If creosote is to hand and is used instead, the barrel *must* be left to weather out of doors for at least six months before being planted, otherwise in warm weather the plants will be killed by the creosote fumes.

Yet another interesting if very small raised garden can be made from an old glazed sink covered with hypertufa. Such a sink can be made to resemble the old stone sinks of our forebears which have now become rarities. It is interesting to note that now that stainless steel sinks are in common use even old glazed sinks are becoming scarce. Should such a glazed sink be available it is advisable to set it in position straight away at the desired height, as sinks are very heavy especially when filled with soil. If the sink is mounted on piles of bricks it should overlap the bricks by 6 in. on all sides, thus partially hiding the bricks and, more important, allowing the feet to go underneath the sink which makes for ease in working.

Once the sink is mounted in position the hypertufa treatment can be done by a person seated in a wheelchair, provided there is good hand and arm ability. Firstly, have a low table placed near the sink, (cover it with newspaper if the surface is precious) and on it place the necessary materials for use. The following will be needed: some Unibond or Polybond, equal quantities of sand (builder's), peat, and cement, an old bowl, some washing-up liquid, a paint brush, a stippling brush, trowel, or rubber glove, and some water.

Commence by washing the sink thoroughly with water and washing-up liquid to remove all traces of grease and dirt. When dry apply the Unibond or Polybond to the sink with a paint brush, sometimes two coats are needed. While the bond is becoming tacky mix the sand, peat and cement together with enough water to make a stiff mix; if it becomes too wet add more dry cement. This mixture is then applied with a trowel or gloved hand to the surfaces of the sink which will be exposed when it is filled with soil. Leave a rough surface by using the stippling brush or similar tool. Do not forget to treat inside the overflow to a depth of 3 in. The final touch can be that of painting over the treated surfaces with milk, this will assist algae and mosses to grow and give a natural appearance. Do not allow the hypertufa to dry out too quickly otherwise it will end up a hard grey colour which will never mellow. If it dries out slowly, taking at least a week, the result will be an attractive brown shade.

When filling the sink with soil cover the outlet with a wire saucepan cleaner for drainage. It is also a good idea to insert a piece of ½ in. metal pipe to half the depth of the soil and allow it to project ½ in. above the soil surface. Sinks are deep and such a pipe will allow the lower level of soil to be watered easily. Place this pipe the opposite end of the sink to the plug-hole.

Recent Developments

There is a great deal of interest being taken at the present time in various aids and appliances designed to make gardening easier and more attractive to the disabled. The tool manufacturers and others continually come up with bright ideas to take all the backache out of the more laborious tasks. A number of these will no doubt find acceptance and fit in with those already described as standard items of equipment for the disabled gardener. Whether such tools and appliances will find acceptance and come into general use will depend largely upon cost and durability.

Among the new ideas that have taken shape in a tangible form recently are:

The Bath Planter Severely handicapped persons cannot work at a raised bed when seated at the side of it so that they are obliged to reach out either to their right or left and do everything from a sideways position. More operations could be carried out if it were possible to have the work area directly in front of the body. Ideally it should be possible for a wheelchair to be positioned to allow the occupant's legs to go underneath the raised garden as when seated at a table. This concept imposes some problems which appear difficult to solve; for example, can there be sufficient depth of soil in the raised bed for plants to grow in and at the same time allow the gardener to work from a sitting position without having to raise the arms high thus causing much stress and strain? If a very shallow depth of soil is provided would this not dry out very quickly in hot weather demanding constant watering? Would not very shallow soil be flooded and waterlogged quickly in very wet weather, and the consequent drainage wet the legs of the gardener? The Bath Planter has been designed at Bath University with a view to overcoming these problems. It has been patented (1976) but is not yet on the market. The table-top planter tray is constructed of glass-fibre, measures 4 feet by 4 feet by 4 in.; it sits upon a metal framed table and is suitable for use when stood upon a firm level surface either in a greenhouse or out of doors. The plants grow in a specially designed peat and bark compost to which basic amounts of plant nutrient have been added. The table-top planter tray is irrigated from beneath through a ¼ in. diameter flexible plastic pipe, connected by an adaptor to the mains supply. Special drainage points have been designed to prevent the compost from becoming flooded during heavy rains and remaining waterlogged for long periods thereafter.

The tray is simple to maintain as there are no complicated parts. The compost is light, clean, and easy to replace. A considerable amount of research into suitable plants to grow in the planter has taken place. The emphasis has been on finding plants that are interesting, fast growing and quick to produce their 'crop' whether flowers or edible parts. In order that the plants shall not tower above the seated person only those with a maximum height of 9 in. have been studied.

Vegetables have proved most successful; excellent crops of lettuce, radish, baby beet, round carrots, silver skinned onions, and bush tomatoes have been grown. Work with flowers has been less detailed, however, the annuals seen most promising and an extremely colourful display of African marigolds produced a mass of colour.

The planter can also be very easily modified to become a capillary bench for container plants. In the spring seedlings and transplants of vegetables and flowers have been grown up to planting out stage. A wide range of containers including both plastic and wooden seed trays and plastic, earthenware, peat, and Polybag pots were tested. All gave good results.

Help would be needed in setting up this table-top planter and filling it with compost and making the necessary connection to the mains water supply. After this the gardener can feel independent and able to grow vegetables and flowers as he wishes.

Other ideas from the University of Bath are (a) to have D-shaped handles screwed with the aid of rawplugs along or into the top of the brick wall of a raised bed to enable people to hang on with one hand while working with the other and (b) to use leaning posts in a line along the front of a raised bed to enable people to jam themselves into the corner between the wall of the bed and the post, leaving both hands free to work.

Rosum Easygrow raised bed This is obtainable through the Gardens for Disabled Trust. It is made in sections of fibre-glass and the units are bolted together with interior strengthening. It may be obtained in different sizes from 5 feet 6 in. by 4 feet to 17 feet by 4 feet, the latter very useful for vegetable crops. It is designed so that it can be worked comfortably from a wheelchair or a garden stool. It has 4 in. depth of soil at the edge, and 18 in. at the centre. Rubble at the base takes the drainage through to the paving beneath.

Car-wheel and tyre container An attractive and efficient plant container can be made from old discarded car wheels with tyre (tubeless and cross-ply) intact. These can be obtained complete from car breakers' yards for £1 to £2 (1977). The wheel and tyre are laid flat on the ground, valve side downward, and the tyre wall is cut round at a distance of 2 in. from the wheel rim. The wheel and tyre are then turned over and by inserting the fingers inside the cut tyre wall this is pulled upward until the tyre is virtually inside-out. The canvas side is now the outside and when painted with Sandtex paint resembles stoneware. Sandtex cannot be purchased in very small quantities and to save waste several containers could be made at one time, sharing with others if necessary. Sandtex gives a better finish than emulsion paint. Thin walled tyres are easier to turn than thick.

Tools If the right tool is available, much work can be done on ground level beds from a sitting position. Most gardeners have a favourite tool which is used in preference to all others. The Disabled Living Foundation have two demonstration gardens for elderly and disabled people; one is at Battersea Park, London and the other at Syon Park, Brentford. These gardens serve to demonstrate both raised beds and suitable gardening tools for handicapped people. Persons visiting these gardens (by appointment) are able to try out the tools (see chapter 12). Some people need very light tools with a handle no longer than 3 feet, some prefer a handle of 5 feet, while others must have thick handles in order to obtain a firm grip. Hoes vary in shape and action; there is the Wilkinson Swoe which is excellent provided perfect control is maintained, the Wolf Push-Pull weeder, which as its name implies

33

can be used with both pushing and pulling action, (this tool also has guards at the sides which prevents plants from being accidentally damaged if the hands are unsteady, and is a good tool for those suffering from spasticity). The Bestwaye weeder described previously, can be used from a sitting position. The Baronet weeder is more like a walking stick with a lever at the handle. The spear shaped end of the weeder is pushed into the soil alongside a weed, the lever is pressed and the tool grips the weed which is then pulled out. This is a good tool for deep rooted weeds and must be used close to the operator, while the Bestwaye weeder is more useful for removing shallow rooted annual weeds at a greater distance.

For the one-handed person unable to dig, the soil miller is a useful tool, while for the raised bed Wolf mini tools on a 1 foot long handle are ideal. Bestwaye also have a weeder on a short handle suitable for a raised bed. The handle-grip (Wolf) is yet another invaluable aid for certain disabilities; a professional gardener who was hemiplegic (on the left side) following a stroke was able to continue digging one-handedly with this appliance attached to his fork — a great deal of determination was also necessary! A most useful article to have in the garden is the Easi-kneeler stool, useful to kneel on when working, with side pieces to lever oneself up with, reversed it becomes a stool to sit on, or can be used as a small table to take cuttings on.

The Anita-grab and the Backsaver are both most helpful in picking up rubbish without bending. With the Baronet long-handled cut-and-hold flower gatherer, flowers or deadheads may be cut off with the use of only one hand while the flower stalk remains in the grip of the cutter. A knife becomes a very precious tool for a gardener; fitting comfortably in the hand, it almost becomes an extension of the hand itself. For a gardener who can only use one hand a knife is almost impossible to open, or if hands are shaky cuts to the flesh are likely. Stanley's retractable bladed pocket knife No.10-959 is more than useful, though it is not strictly a garden knife. Blades are replaceable and Nos. 5904 and 5905 are the best for garden use. The Ceka ratchet florian pruner is a very light secateur weighing only 4½ oz. This pruner, working on a ratchet principle, cuts wood up to 1 in. in diameter, and does not need a great deal of pressure, which is useful when the grip is weak.

Each tool has its own particular use, and what suits one person may not suit another. Tools will continue to be mentioned throughout the book whenever they are considered to be useful.

3   Hedges and Fences

The thought of hedge trimming is often so daunting that the gardener promptly chooses a fence instead. In some cases a fence is the only answer, particularly if complete privacy is needed. However, although a fence has its advantages, a living hedge can do much more to enhance the beauty of a garden. Hedges filter the wind through their growth, diminishing its strength by the time it reaches the garden, whereas the force of the wind builds up against a solid fence or wall, then flows over the top creating air turbulence amongst the plants on the other side and often wrecking them.

The final decision however does lie with the gardener, knowing what he can or cannot manage. A hedge does not necessarily have to be a formal, clipped affair. An informal hedge of shrubs chosen because they need little pruning can often be cared for by a handicapped person.

The greatest difficulty for any gardener who is elderly or disabled is to inherit a garden that already has a boundary of formal hedges, especially if they are of privet. Privet is often used in towns and suburbs because it withstands pollution and is green all the winter but it needs clipping several times a year, which is very tiring even with an electric hedge trimmer. Every so often privet has also to be cut hard back at the sides because it has become too broad to manage. This cutting back has to be right into the old wood using secateurs or possibly a saw, which weak hands and arms cannot manage. Not only is the regular care demanding, privet is also a hungry feeder; it has been said nothing should be planted within at least 5 feet of it (remembering that area has to be kept weeded). Certainly vegetables growing within 3 feet of a privet hedge are nowhere near as large or healthy as those in the remainder of the row.

To take a privet hedge out would be very hard work, or costly to have done by outside labour. There would also be the further expense of planting a new hedge or erecting a fence. There is however a method of alteration, albeit rather slow. This is by planting holly seedlings or young holly plants in the gaps at the base of the hedge. If there are no gaps then these can be made by cutting back the privet to form arches about 18 in. wide at the base and about 2 feet high. Holly does not grow well in heavy clay, it likes a well drained soil, and older plants do not transplant well, but seedlings and small plants in well drained soil will grow and hold their own with privet. As the holly grows so the privet is cut back further and further on either side of it, until a privet bush can be taken out altogether. It is best to use the common holly *Ilex aquifolium* for this planting; when large enough this will set fruit, giving more seedlings for planting up further gaps. When fully grown holly needs only one clip a year as a formal hedge.

Hawthorn is another hedge often seen, especially in country gardens. It is attractive and birds like it for nesting, while at the base wild flowers such as primroses and violets can grow. An old book says the Elizabethans grew such hedges by stretching a piece of rope along the length required. Into this rope the haws of a hawthorn were pushed. Both the leathery coat of the haws and the rope rotted in the winter, while the weathered and released seeds germinated in the spring. Hawthorn needs several clips per year, and every so often there is the heavy work of taking out dead wood in winter, often in inclement weather. Hollies can also be insinuated gradually into hawthorn hedges as well as privet. This method has been tried out practically with great success on a fairly light, well-drained soil.

If formal hedges are especially desired, the easiest to manage are yew and holly; they grow slowly on maturing once they are established and are therefore more easy of control, only needing one clip per year, though with holly of course one has prickles to contend with. Yew makes an excellent foil for plants, but it should not be used in the country where there are cattle, as it is poisonous to stock.

If new hedges are being planted, they need just as much care as any shrub in the garden, with dug soil free of weeds and fertiliser added. Spacing of formal hedging plants has a bearing on the ultimate height of the hedge. The closer together the hedge plants are placed the shorter the final height of the hedge will be.

Those that are planted far apart will produce a taller hedge. There is nowadays a garden service in some areas that will clip hedges and mow lawns.

There are other ways of having an attractive boundary round a garden other than a formal hedge, such as informal hedges; groupings of shrubs in front of a wire-netting fence; ivies climbing over a fence; or a low double wall with dwarf shrubs growing in the bed between the walls.

Informal Hedge

These hedges are far easier to manage than the formal ones, but once again it is advisable to choose the slower growing shrubs, for strong growing ones can soon get out-of-hand and look thoroughly untidy; worse still they might overhang or partially block a pathway, causing a mobility hazard.

For an informal hedge the same species of shrub is chosen throughout. There is no hedge clipping as such, but a limited amount of pruning of the shrubs may be necessary. If a species of shrub is chosen which needs little pruning throughout its life, then the hedge will be far easier to manage. In a garden where there has to be much paving the general appearance can be rather hard but an informal hedge along the boundary can counterbalance this.

Some of the shrubs which can be used bear flowers followed by attractive fruit; this is an incentive for birds to visit the garden. The waxwing, a rather rare winter visitor, has been seen in town gardens as well as in the country, brightening up a cotoneaster hedge as it alights for the fruits. In really cold weather redwings will come into even small gardens for any fruits.

Of the shrubs which lose their leaves in winter *Chaenomeles speciosa* better known as 'Cydonia' or just 'Japonica', (flowering quince) makes a good hedge. It is used for this purpose in the United States, but in the British Isles seems mainly used as an individual shrub. As a hedge it will need some cutting occasionally, preferably in winter; however it still bears blossom well if left unpruned and is a lovely sight in early spring. This shrub grows slowly (though there is some dependence on types of soils) and so can be kept under control without a great deal of work. The flowers are followed by thick green foliage and in many seasons fruit.

Berberis and pyracantha are often recommended for informal hedges, but are not really suitable for anyone with a disability. They are inclined to grow too strongly and berberis have strong spines which can even probe clothing. When grown en masse berberis tend to make an unmanageable thicket.

COTONEASTER DIVARICATUS is deciduous but has good autumn colour as well as fruits. It grows to about 5 feet and is planted 2 feet apart. *C.simonsii* is semi-evergreen but has scarlet berries which often persist until the spring. It can grow very tall eventually. Planting distance is 2 feet for this also.

ELAEAGNUS PUNGENS is an evergreen with leaves shining green above and whitish underneath: it is rather spreading, but because of its vigorous habit it makes a good windbreak for a garden in an exposed position. It does grow quite tall so that help might be needed in cutting back every fourth year or so. Planting distance is 3 feet. *E.pungens* 'Maculata' is evergreen but the leaves have a central splash of gold, which gives a most cheerful look in winter. It is a very handsome shrub of moderate growth, easy to control with only the occasional cut-back of an odd shoot. It is not quite so resistant as *E. pungens* mentioned above and gives better results where there is some natural shelter. Planting distance 2½ feet.

FUCHSIA MAGELLANICA 'Gracilis' and *F.riccartonii* are both fuchsias suitable for hedging in mild localities.

OLEARIA HAASTII, known as the 'Daisy bush', bears fragrant

daisy-like flowers in July-August. It is very tolerant of most conditions including towns and the seaside; by the latter it grows particularly well. Should the shrubs in the hedge become straggly after several years, they can be cut back into hard wood; help may be needed for this, otherwise there is no pruning.

RHODODENDRONS Where a garden has a peat soil rhododendrons make a good informal hedge, but the large types must be avoided, particularly *R.ponticum* the common purple one, as it spreads easily and becomes unmanageable. *R.myrtifolium* has a compact habit of growth to about 5 feet, flowering in May-June. Planting distance 2 feet. Various other rhododendrons may be found in catalogues.

ROSMARINUS OFFICINALIS rosemary, makes a very good informal hedge if the fastigiate form 'Jessups' Upright' is chosen. The plants will grow to 5 feet. If it is possible to give a light clip after flowering the shrubs keeps more dense.

ULEX EUROPEUS 'Plena' is the double flowered gorse which is a shrub for very poor soils. The common gorse of our moorlands throws out suckers and would soon be all over the garden. The double flowered form remains compact, though it can become quite large in girth, and of course is prickly. Gorse is a glorious mass of bloom in spring with a scent rather like coconut. It needs no attention for most years, but after several years it may become leggy and can be cut hard back in April. Some members of a youth group might be of assistance with this.

Fencing with shrubs

An attractive way of making a boundary to the garden and integrating it with the various plantings, it to put up a low wire-netting fence. This legally defines the property and keeps out inquisitive dogs (cats are another matter!). In front of this netting fence may be grown shrubs in irregular groups which, if well placed, can give the illusion of the garden leading on to somewhere further. Evergreens and conifers can be mixed with some deciduous shrubs to give the fresh young green of spring.

The choice of shrubs will depend on the individual, but

those which need little or no pruning are the wisest choice. It may take quite a time before this border begins to assert itself and becomes part of the garden, for, it should be remembered, shrubs that grow quickly are the ones that need most cutting and keeping under control. The slow-growing types need far less attention even when fully grown. If a path is made along the edge of this shrub border, the other side of the path could continue with a border of flowers. Details of shrubs are given in chapter 4.

Fence with ivies

The last type of hedge to be mentioned, which is easy to manage, is a chestnut paling or trellis fence over which ivies are grown. This is particularly neat and attractive for a small area. Quite a number of different ivies may be grown, from dark to light green, also the variegated. Ivies are so often left to grow as they will that the cutting-back in April becomes a difficult operation because the wood has become thick and old and hard to cut. The best method of upkeep is to cut back any shoot which has grown out too far while the stem is still soft. This can be done whenever one is in the garden; there will be times when there are no shoots at all to cut, but this way management is spread over a long period, with the minimum of effort used as the wood never becomes really old and hard, except that which is close to the fence, and forms the framework. Birds love ivy for roosting in, especially the little wren. This fence-cum-ivy can be made to whatever height is desired. A firm path is needed alongside, but again flowers can border the other side of the path with the ivy providing a good background.

Double wall with plantings

If a double wall is made with the walls 18 in. high and about 15 in. apart, the intervening space can be filled with soil. This makes an excellent raised bed, as well as forming a boundary. If a low hedge is required along the top of this double wall, *Mahonia aquifolia* is excellent for the purpose; it does not grow too tall, is attractive and can easily be kept

41

under control as necessary.

Fences

There are times, and places, where fences are essential. They have certain advantages over hedges in giving complete privacy immediately upon erection, especially near the house. For the person who has no alternative but to stand while gardening, fences make excellent frames for climbing plants, espalier fruit trees etc., which can make the garden both decorative and varied.

Fences are expensive so quite a deal of thought and planning should be done before deciding on what to erect. The choice also depends on whether the fencing is eventually not seen because of shrubs growing in front of it, or whether it is to be a feature with plants trained on it. 5 or 6 foot fencing could be used nearest the house with lower fencing further down the garden, or giving way to an informal hedge.

Some fences will filter the wind, for example the interwoven panel fence, and wattle hurdles. Though the most attractive, wattle hurdles do tend to become brittle after a time, with pieces breaking off, particularly after long spells of dry weather.

A trellis type fence which can be used as it is or with ivy growing over it as previously described, is the X-panda fencing which is simple to erect. It is sold in packs at shops and garden centres, and can be taken home in the boot of a car. Upright posts to which the fencing is fixed are also available. The value of this fence is not only in its easy erection but in that it can be stretched out to a greater length where desired with diminishing height. The size of the pack is 57 in. by 9 in. by 5 in. and the variations of height can be as follows:

    4 feet high 8 feet long
    3 ft 3 in high 10 feet long
    2 ft 6 in high 12 feet long
    1 ft 9 in high 14 ft 6 in. long

The makers are willing to send these packs and uprights direct by national carriers for the extra cost involved, for those who are unable to visit a garden centre. Details are given in chapter 12. This type of fencing could be put up by those people whose disability is slight. Directions for erection are given with each pack.

Cleft chestnut fencing has a long life and is sold in rolls, usually about 10 yds per roll. A 3 foot high fence with 3 in. spacing between palings could be used for covering with ivy like the X-panda trellis and at this height could be managed by a person in a wheelchair.

4   Trees and Shrubs

Plants are what gardening is all about. While previous chapters have dealt with various mechanical and practical aids, it should not be forgotten that plants can be aids in themselves if easy care ones are chosen. Often we inherit gardens with beautiful plants in them, but they are of little use if too difficult to care for; for example, climbing roses over an archway are unsuitable when the gardener is in a wheelchair, or for an ambulant person when the climbing of a step-ladder is completely impossible.

Plantings also need thinking about by those who have retired. That which can be tackled at the time of planting may present problems several years later. It is far more satisfactory to look out on to an 'easy care' garden which although not strictly neat and tidy is pleasant to look at, than on to a formally planted garden which ought to be neat and tidy, but is very much the opposite and crying out for attention.

This and the following chapter will deal with plants to be grown both at ground level and in raised beds, plants which possess qualities valuable to the gardener who has limited physical ability. It also tries to deal with the different aspects of growing, such as soil conditions, position of garden — whether in sun or shade, rainfall and exposure to winds and frosts, which make for individuality. No two gardens are alike and a book can only give guidelines.

One of the most difficult of gardens to work in is that which has a heavy clay soil. There are chemical aids such as

using Breakthrough. Another way this obstacle may be overcome is by having a slightly raised bed of about 15 in. containing easily workable soil. Many plants thrive in a clay soil
once their roots have penetrated into it, it is the initial planting which is difficult. A shallow raised bed will give the right
planting conditions for the gardener who likes gardening at
ground level.

Ease of cultivation is all important and if moving house
(unless the gardener is using raised beds entirely) the aim
should be to choose a house with a garden with soil which is
sandy or gravelly i.e. 'light' soil as opposed to the 'heavy' soil
of a sticky clay; it is true that a light soil tends to dry out in
hot weather, but it is easy to work.

Trees

So many of our smaller gardens lack trees. When there have
been consecutive summers of grey skies and rain, people feel
they need all the sunshine they can get, but when a really hot
summer comes, they find they cannot work or even sit in the
garden because there is no shade. Besides giving shade trees
are beautiful in themselves, the grace of their growth, the
colour of the leaves changing from spring through to
autumn, and then the network of bare branches against a
winter sky, while winter sunlight on the bark does much to
enhance the garden. The light and shade through a tree gives
charm to the surroundings, with dappled light on patio and
paving, but the right tree must be chosen, so that it adds to
the scene rather than dominates it.

The flowering crab apple is a favourite tree, and unlike the
flowering cherry it usually sets fruit; this can be a hazard
when the fruit falls on a path, as if they become squashed
and slippery, they will make walking dangerous. Such a tree
is best planted out of harm's way at the back of a bed where
it can still be seen and admired, particularly when blackbirds
or redwings come to enjoy its crop.

Occasionally a garden will have too many trees, or trees
that are too large; these can make the garden gloomy, especially if they are conifers. If possible some of the trees are
better felled, but the work of a tree-feller is expensive, due in

large measure to their heavy accident insurance.

When planting new trees, it is best to avoid planting conifers near the house, for they tend to become depressing. Planted at a distance they are trees of great beauty, giving warmth in winter. The trees which are given in the following pages have been chosen mainly for growing in small gardens. Where large gardens are concerned, the selection is wide, but when buying for a small garden it is necessary to envisage how large a tree will become. A tree can too easily take over the whole garden.

ACER, the maples. Most of the acers make large trees but varieties of the Japanese maple *Acer palmatum* are dwarf and take several years to grow large enough to give any shade. They are trees in miniature and none the less lovely for that, beautiful in both form and colour. A variety that is usually easily available and most brilliant in autumn colour is *A.palmatum* 'Osakazuki'.

CRATAEGUS Our common hawthorn is in the genus crataegus; it is a very 'English' tree which as it grows older develops an interesting stem. Types usually grown in the garden are varieties of *C.oxycantha* with either red or pink flowers. The red varieties take several years before they have much bloom, but are most rewarding when they do bloom. Crataegus make small trees suitable for most gardens. *C.oxycantha* 'Paul's Scarlet' is double flowered as is *C.o.* 'Rosea flore pleno'.

C.ARNOLDIANA is a beautiful small tree bearing white flowers followed by large red fruits; *C.lavallei* is a small tree with a dense head. The leaves are darkish green turning orange-brown in autumn and often persisting until December. The fruits which are large and orange-red also persist well in to the winter so they are not troublesome on a path in autumn.

ELAEAGNUS ANGUSTIFOLIA, the oleaster, makes a very small tree, sometimes only a large shrub, so that the lower growths have to be cut out to form a clear main stem. It is a dainty tree, with grey-green willow-like leaves silver on the reverse, and bears small fragrant flowers in June.

GLEDITSIA TRIACANTHOS 'Sunburst' is the Honey Locust tree. This is medium sized so is not for the very small garden. The attractive divided leaves of this variety are bright yellow in the spring and most arresting. This tree is useful in towns as it withstands pollution well.

MALUS, the flowering crab apple. *Malus* 'Golden Hornet' is a smallish tree of upright growth and has white flowers in the spring. Its main attraction is in the autumn when it bears a heavy crop of yellow fruits which persist until late in the year if the blackbirds leave them alone. It is however lovely in winter to see two or three cock blackbirds among the bright yellow fruits, especially if backed by a blue sky. This tree needs to be planted within sight of a window.

The prunus is a very large genus including the peach and almond and the flowering plums and cherries. The peach and almond, though lovely, are best avoided, as they are susceptible to a disease which curls the leaves; this is unsightly and becomes a worry.

Two of the many flowering plum trees are particularly attractive, and are usually easily available, also they do not set fruit so may overhang paths or paving. *Prunus cerasifera* 'Pissardii' is the purple leaved plum and *P.c.* 'Nigra' has stems and leaves of blackish purple. Both are small trees with white or pinkish white flowers in March/April and are attractive throughout the year because of their coloured foliage. *P.blireana* is a beautiful small tree of the plum group. Its leaves are coppery purple and are out when the double pink flowers bloom in April.

Of the Japanese cherries *Prunus* 'Amanogawa' is an erect tree like a miniature Lombardy poplar in shape. It takes up very little space, but does not afford much shade. It would be most attractive in a small paved garden.

SALIX Willows on the whole are too large for small gardens, but there is a variety of the common willow weeping in form, which stays quite small; this is *Salix caprea* 'Pendula'.

Small conifers are difficult to suggest. The dwarf ones are very slow growing indeed, but there are a few of medium height with not too much spread.

CHAEMAECYPARIS LAWSONIANA 'Fletcheri' grows to about 15 feet and has feathery grey-green foliage with columnar habit; it is an attractive tree and well worth growing.

CRYPTOMERIA JAPONICA 'Elegans' is a long name for a very beautiful tree that has a dense billowing type of growth which turns a bronzy-red in winter warm-looking whatever the weather, but a true delight when the winter sun shines on it. It does grow to about 20 feet and is thick through, so needs space for development. There is a variety 'Nana' which is more dwarf, and is sometimes obtainable.

JUNIPERUS COMMUNIS 'Hibernica', or Irish juniper, looks very well in a formal setting such as a paved area. It forms a dense column of about 2 feet in width and grows to about 9 feet. It has a blue-grey sheen and is very attractive.

JUNIPERUS VIRGINIANA 'Skyrocket's' name describes the tree perfectly for it is a pencil shape and even when grown to 15 feet high is only about 1 foot in width. Where the area paved for easy maintenance is not very large, this tree gives height without taking up space, and is most effective. All junipers like lime in the soil, which can be added, except where there is natural peat.

Shrubs

The old-fashioned shrubbery seemed a dreary kind of place with dark evergreens and little to relieve the monotony. There is today a very wide variety of shrubs available. including those grown for ground cover; taller ones can be grown in mixed borders with perennials bulbs and annuals. Many shrubs have beautiful flowers as well as an attractive habit of growth and good leaf-form; but the first thing a person with a handicap has to think of when choosing shrubs is 'Can I manage the care of them?' 'What pruning may they need?' so any choice will be limited by what can be managed before it is considered if the shrubs are suitable for the soil and general conditions of the particular garden they are being chosen for.

Planting

Before listing varieties of shrubs that are fairly easy to care for, a note must be made on planting. If a person has a handicap which prevents him doing the planting himself, he at least should know what to do, so as to direct operations. A badly planted shrub can soon be a dead one, which one can ill-afford these days. Depth of planting will be the same as it was at the nursery or garden centre; a mark on the stem will show how deep it should be planted. The hole for the plant needs to be amply wide enough to take the plant, and for free roots to spread out without being cramped; peat mixed with the soil to go round the roots helps the plant to make a good start. Firm planting is essential. Container grown plants are of course much simpler to plant out and depth of planting will be obvious.

The following list of shrubs may seem somewhat limited; if, however, pruning can be managed, then a far wider choice may be made. Well known shrubs such as forsythia and mock-orange have not been included as they require pruning every year, sometimes cutting into old wood which can be difficult. Stress has therefore been laid on those shrubs which need little or no pruning, or maybe only a cutting back once in every four or five years, when it should be possible to obtain help which probably could not be obtained every year.

ARTEMESIA ABROTANUM, the Southernwood or 'Lad's Love', has been cultivated in cottage gardens in England since the sixteenth century. It grows to about 4 feet and has finely divided aromatic grey-green leaves. Any straggling growth which occurs will need cutting back occasionally, but if cut while growth is still soft it is easy to manage with a long-handled flower cutter. This plant likes a light soil and a sunny spot. It can succumb to heavy winter wet.

AUCUBA JAPONICA is usually grown in the variegated form and is known as the spotted laurel. It will grow almost anywhere, whether in sun or in dense shade, and is not particular as to soil or pollution in towns. Sunlight does however light up the leaves and make it look its best, especially in winter. It can be cut back hard in April if it outgrows its bounds. It is slow growing unlike the common laurel. The spotted laurel is useful for screening.

BERBERIS All berberis have prickles, so gloves need to be worn when handling this shrub. Berberis are easy to grow, thriving in most garden soils, as long as there is no water-logging, They will grow in entire shade but do prefer some sunshine. Transplanting is best done when small as larger plants do not 'take' well. After transplanting many varieties will lose their leaves, but, given time, new growth will break from the base.

Some species are evergreen, other deciduous. Of the evergreen species *B.darwinii* is the earliest to flower. Its brilliant orange flowers are very handsome against the dark shining foliage. This plant was discovered in Chile by Charles Darwin in 1835. No regular pruning is necessary, but a drastic cut back when it is getting too large (it can grow to 10 feet); this can be done after flowering.

B.STENOPHYLLA is another evergreen berberis with smaller leaves and dense growth which arches downwards bearing yellow flowers in spring. It requires pruning as for *B.darwinii*.

B.GAGNEPAINII from West China has fresh green pointed leaves with crinkled edges and is known as the 'fernleaf berberis'. It is evergreen and has yellow pendant flowers. Pruning will be as for *B.darwinii*.

B.VERRUCULOSA is also evergreen, but its growth is not as strong as that of the previous berberis mentioned. The dark glossy leaves are silver underneath, and the plant is particularly attractive in winter.

B.THUNBERGII is deciduous and was introduced from Japan. The leaves turn a brilliant colour before they fall in the autumn. The variety *B.t.*'Atropurpurea' has reddish purple leaves throughout the spring and summer. A charming dwarf variety of this is 'Roseglow' which makes an attractive partnership with lavender.

Except for 'Roseglow' berberis are best grown as separate specimens; if two or three grow into one another they make a thicket which is difficult to control.

BUPLEURUM FRUTICOSUM is a shrub which grows to about 5 feet and needs no pruning. The leaves are bluish green and the small yellow flowers appear in late summer. Its great asset is that it will grow in exposed places, particularly near the sea, and so makes a good shelter for other plants. It also thrives on chalky soils.

THE CAMELLIA is a well-known and beautiful early-flowering shrub and is not as delicate as is often thought. The plant itself is quite hardy, but as the flowers appear early in the year, they can indeed be soon frosted; these shrubs are therefore best grown against a fence or wall facing north or west, as if facing east, the sun catching them while frost is still on them will damage and brown the flowers. If in the semi-shade of trees they can be grown in the open instead of by a wall. Camellias like an acid condition of soil but are a little more lime-tolerant than rhododendrons. They are particularly good for growing in tubs. The best types for general planting are those of the hybrid *C.* x *williamsii* and the species *C.japonica*. The leaves of *Camellia thea* give us the tea we drink. No pruning is required at all for camellias.

CERATOSTIGMA is a lovely sub-shrub from China. It may die back during the winter, but will shoot again from the base in the spring making about 3 feet of growth and forming a thick clump of individual shoots which in early August will bear brilliant blue flowers. The flowers continue until October when the leaves turn an attractive red. Pruning is by cutting back any dead growth there is in March. This growth is very thin and not difficult to cut.

CHAENOMELES has already been mentioned in the chapter on hedging plants. It is often known as just 'japonica'. The different species and varieties make fine flowering shrubs which will grow in most soils and flower in sun or shade, and do not require regular pruning. They can in fact be left unpruned but then must be given more space when planted out. Before buying, the species should be checked as some grow rather tall. *C.japonica* is quite a small shrub, but *C.lagenaria* with varieties of lovely colours is medium sized and rather spreading, so needs room if it is left unpruned.

CHOISYA TERNATA, the Mexican Orange, is a bushy ever-green shrub with trifoliate leaves. It bears white flowers similar to orange blossom in June and again in October/November if the weather is favourable. It is listed as 'not quite hardy' but it has been known to withstand very cold winters. It is the cold winds that it dislikes, and it grows best where there is protection from north and east winds. Choisya grows in sun or shade and thrives in industrial towns. Should it become too big (which will take a long time) it can have a clip back in April, otherwise no pruning is necessary.

COTINUS COGGYGRIA, the Smoke Bush, has a purple leaved

form which is the one most often seen. It makes a spreading bush 10 feet wide and as high, but is worth having if there is room. The panicles of flowers look like puffs of smoke against the rounded purple leaves, which turn yellow and crimson in autumn. Cotinus needs no pruning but likes a well drained soil and sunny position.

ELAEAGNUS. One of the most attractive of the elaeagnus is *E.pungens* 'Maculata'. Growth is moderate, up to 10 feet in height and nearly as broad. This elaeagnus is evergreen with bright splashes of gold in the centre of the leaves. It is easy to grow if it is given protection from cold winds in the early stages. No pruning is required but any plain green shoots which appear must be cut out.

EUONYMUS There are two groups of this shrub quite distinct from one another. *E.europaeus* is the wild spindle tree, deciduous, with brilliant fruits in autumn. It grows on chalk hills. In the garden it needs no pruning but has the drawback of being host in winter to the blackfly which infests broad beans. The other group consists of evergreen shrubs from Japan: *E.japonicus* has shining green leaves and there are also variegated forms. These do grow rather large but are mentioned here as they stand salt spray better than most shrubs and make good shelter for other plants in gardens by the sea.

FATSIA JAPONICA is another shrub which can grow large but also can be reduced in size in April when it is necessary. It has very large, deeply lobed leaves and sprays of white flowers early in winter. It has a somewhat exotic appearance yet it is very tough and quite hardy and will even grow in the areas of London houses.

FUCHSIA Most fuchsias are half hardy and are 'bedded out' each year, but there are several which are perfectly hardy, and when buying plants it must be made quite sure that a hardy variety has been chosen. Old growth has to be cut back in spring, but if done every year it is quite thin and easy to cut. Hardy varieties are 'M'me Cornelissen' which is semi-double and is white and carmine, and 'Mrs Popple' which is carmine and deep violet (and particularly hardy). The species *Fuchsias gracilis* is very hardy with small but dainty flowers.

GENISTA, the brooms, are beautiful shrubs. Most need annual pruning, but there are two which can be left unpruned. *G.aetnensis* 'The Mount Etna bloom' grows very tall eventually and is often treated as a tree. When fully grown it has thin pendulous branches which are covered with pea-like yellow blossoms in July and August. It does not need pruning but when first planted a stake is advisable. It does well in dry rather hungry soil, and because of its ultimate size is only for the larger garden. *G.hispanica* is the Spanish broom (not to be confused with *Spartium junceum* also sometimes called 'Spanish broom') which looks rather like a neat fine-leaved gorse bush. It grows to about 2 feet high and though the bush remains neat spreads to about 4 feet. It is prickly; but as it does not need pruning this is no real problem. It is covered with yellow flowers in spring.

HAMMAMELIS, the witch-hazel. There are two species of this lovely shrub: *H.japonica* is from Japan and *H.mollis* from China; both have several varieties. The individual flowers have thin strap-like petals, sometimes very small, and the colour varies from pale yellow to orange with a purplish centre. There is a profusion of flowers covering the shrub which is most arresting in January sunshine. Some varieties start flowering in autumn while others go on through the winter with the latest ones flowering in March; the majority of flowers are scented. The leaves are oval and turn a good colour in autumn. The hammamelis does need plenty of room for development as it can grow to 12 — 15 feet and can be 12 feet broad. It needs no pruning and looks far better if left untouched; it is really suited to the larger garden and could take the place of a tree. Varieties are *H.japonica* 'Ruby Glow' with reddish gold flowers, and brilliant autumn colour to the leaves, and *H.mollis* 'Pallida', considered the finest witch-hazel, with pale though bright yellow flowers which are sweetly scented.

HEBE Shrubby veronicas. These shrubs come from New Zealand and used to be called veronicas but this name now only applies to the soft-leaved kinds of the flower border which die down in winter. The shrubby types which grow to about 3 - 4 feet according to variety are named 'Hebe' and are most useful shrubs. They need to have shelter in the north and east of the country but do very well in seaside gardens. The smaller narrow-leaved types are the hardiest, all are evergreen and will thrive in most types of soil. *Hebe* 'Majorie' is one of the hardiest; it forms a neat bush and has pale lilac flowers through summer to autumn. *H.cupressoides* has such small leaves that at a first glance it could be mistaken for a conifer; it is starred with tiny mauve flowers in summer. *H.*'Mrs Winder' grows to 3 feet and makes a compact bush with purplish leaves which turn a rich plum colour in winter; the flowers are an attractive blue. *H.albicans* has broad silver grey foliage forming a neat bush of 1-2 feet which produces white flowers. Hebes are 'easy' shrubs and do not need pruning, but should they become 'leggy' or straggly they may be cut back in April except *H.cupressoides*.

HIBISCUS *H.syriacus* is the only hardy form in this country. When in flower it can look quite exotic with its numerous large hollyhock-like flowers, single or double with colours ranging from white through pink and mauve to blue. The variety 'Blue Bird' is especially good. Hibiscus demand a well drained soil and a sunny position. They need neither pruning nor dead heading and can reach a height of 8 feet.

HYDRANGEA Everyone knows the mop-head hydrangea. True, to obtain the best effect it requires pruning, but it still gives a show without, though the whole bush does become rather tall and thick. It is good for damp situations. It is not recommended particularly but if it is already in the garden it can be left to see how it behaves. The flowers die gracefully and are attractive for dried flower arrangements.

LAVENDULA, lavender, needs no introduction. It is a shrub that can be used in a mixed border to great effect. Like so many aromatic grey-leaved shrubs it likes a well drained soil and sunny position.

LAVATERIA OLBIA is sometimes referred to as a sub-shrub due to its soft growth, though it can attain a height of 15 feet or more. It is the shrubby mallow and has the typical mallow flowers like those of the wild plant, which appear from July to September; they are mauvish in colour. The best variety is 'Rosea'. Shrubby mallow grows well by the sea and will flourish in most places where the soil is not too moist. It is not considered a 'choice' shrub but grows quickly and gives plenty of colour. No pruning is needed.

MAGNOLIA Most magnolias are too big for the average size garden but the species *Magnolia stellata* is smaller and a delight to see. It is not difficult to grow provided there is no free lime as in a chalk soil. A mulching of leaf-mould or rhododendron peat each spring helps it greatly, especially in the early years of growth. This species comes from Japan and is slow growing, forming a rounded shrub about 10 feet high. The many-petalled white flowers appear in April. It needs no pruning.

MAHONIA This genus used to be among the berberis to which it has some similarity, but there are no prickles and the leaves are larger. The leaves are composed of leaflets holly-like in appearance and they turn a bronzy red in winter, useful in flower decoration. The yellow flowers appear from February to April. This shrub spreads by suckers but the growth is not rapid. *M.aquifolium* is useful for filling the awkward corner, or in hungry soils or under the shade of trees.

MAHONIA 'Charity' is a medium sized shrub of stately habit, very upright in growth. The leaves are about 1 foot long consisting of long spiny leaflets and there are racemes of scented yellow flowers up the main stem which bloom in winter. It is altogether a most handsome plant. *M.japonica* is another good plant, architecturally beautiful growing to 6 feet eventually, with racemes of yellow flowers. It prefers some shade. None of the mahonias need pruning.

OLEARIA *Olearia haastii* is often called the 'Daisy Bush' for the appearance of the small white flowers which appear in July and August. This shrub makes a medium sized bush with small greyish leaves, felted underneath. Not exciting, but quite hardy everywhere and tolerant of both coastal and town conditions. It can have a light trim over in the spring, but this is not essential if it cannot be managed.

POTENTILLA (shrubby) *Potentilla fruticosa* grows wild throughout Europe and is seen in brilliant masses in Co. Clare, Ireland. There it grows to a shrub about 1 foot high, with roots deep down in the crevices of the limestone, spreading its branches with bright yellow flowers over the bare grey rock. It makes a wonderful sight, and is an indication of the plant's needs — cool moisture for the roots and head in full sun. It is a tough little shrub, perfectly hardy and if full sun is not possible will still flower, though flowers are not so numerous. There are several varieties, 'Katherine Dykes' being a favourite and usually obtainable quite easily; this grows to 5 feet and has primrose coloured flowers from July to October. The variety 'Elizabeth' has canary yellow flowers and grows to 3 feet. No pruning is needed with this very well worthwhile shrub.

PYRACANTHA, or firethorn, is for the larger garden as it will grow to 10 feet or more and is better left alone unpruned, for it then flowers more freely in the spring and follows up with brilliant red or orange berries in the autumn. All varieties are hardy and it is one of the best evergreen shrubs, tolerant of most soils and able to withstand winds and town pollution. Some varieties are *P.rogersiana* 'Fructu Luteo' at 10 feet and *P.watereri*, 10 feet.

Rosemary. *R.officinalis* is used for its herbal qualities but makes a good shrub with its small aromatic leaves and light blue flowers. The variety known as 'Miss Jessup' is of upright growth to about 5 feet and does not take up too much room.

SENECIO is a genus that has many members, but the shrub member which is popular is *Senecio laxifolia* often sold as *S.greyii*. It is a soft grey-leaved shrub ideal to cover a wide area in full sun or partial shade. The maximum height is 4 feet but the usual height nearer 3 feet. It sometimes has to be restricted by cutting back in spring, but this is usually not difficult as the wood is fairly soft.

SIPHONOSMANTHUS DELAVAYII is an evergreen shrub from China. It has small leaves, dark green and shining, with small white fragrant flowers in April. It will grow in most soils in sun or partial shade and needs no pruning.

SYRINGA, lilac. Most lilacs are large and difficult to dead-head and care for generally but the Korean lilac *Syringa velutina (palibiana)* makes a smaller compact shrub that is often used in the larger rock gardens. It has flowers of lilac-rose and is suitable for a small garden. The dead-heading can be done with a long-armed flower gatherer if wished.

ULEX, gorse. *Ulex europeus* 'Plenus' is the double flowered gorse; it makes a splendid shrub where the soil is poor and dry and acid. It does not sucker like the common single-flowered gorse, but remains compact (though rather large) and needs no pruning. It grows to about 5 feet, is thick through and is a blaze of colour in April/May.

VIBURNUM There are several species of viburnum, the native one of the chalk hills is the wayfaring tree. The most widely grown garden species is *Viburnum tinus* often known as 'Laurestinus'. This is an evergreen bush which will grow 7-10 feet and become very thick too, but it never becomes leggy; there are always leaves to the base. When too big (which will take several years) it can be cut back in April then left for many years before another cut. It has white flowers which are often out for Christmas and will go on flowering through January until the spring. It will grow in complete shade as well as sun and is one of our most tolerant shrubs. *V.opulus* is the guelder rose which has white flowers followed in autumn by fruits that are translucent red. It likes wet conditions and is suitable for a garden where there is boggy land. *V.farreri (fragrans)* is a medium sized shrub which is rather stiff and erect. The clusters of white flowers, pink in bud, appear before the leaves in early spring and are sweetly scented which is the shrub's main attraction. No special pruning is needed. *V.bodnantense* is similar but makes a finer specimen and the sweetly scented pink flowers appear from November onwards, being frost resistant. While a better plant it does grow bigger than *V.farreri*.

Shrubs for Acid Soils and Raised Peat Beds

Rhododendrons and heathers are associated with acid soils, and they are splendid plants. Heathers are not only beautiful, but also make good ground cover plants (chapter 7) and rhododendrons provide a regular blaze of glory. Rhododendrons flower better when dead-headed each year, so that when buying, the ultimate size of the plant needs to be considered. The type chosen must be within the scope of the gardener who is to do this job.

Heathers are better for a clip over once a year, but still

give good colour if this cannot be managed and are well worth growing.

There are three main groups of heathers: calluna, which is the commonest and grows on our heaths and moorlands, is known as 'ling' in England and heather in Scotland; daboecia, the Irish heath; and the various species of erica, known as bell heather. The selection of plants which follows has been chosen for giving colour all the year round in the peat garden or raised peat bed.

CALLUNA VULGARIS 'Golden Feather' is a non-flowering variety grown for its foliage which is a bright golden yellow in summer changing to orange red in winter. *C.v.* 'Beoly Gold' has white flowers in August-September but is also grown for its good golden foliage all the year round. *C.v.* 'David Eason' has reddish flowers in September/November with light green foliage. It is a very good late flowering variety.

DABOECIA CANTABRICA All the varieties of this plant flower continuously from June to October. Plants can become rather bushy and may get too big for a small raised peat bed; the leaves are larger than in the ordinary heather while the loose racemes of bells hang from wiry stems 10 in. long. *Daboecia cantabrica* 'Atropurpurea' has deep purple flowers, and *D.c.* 'Donard pink' has delicate pink flowers. The latter variety has a more upright habit of growth so would not be too big for the raised bed.

ERICA CARNEA is the winter flowering heath and its varieties are named in chapter 7. *E.erigena* will grow on lime soils like the *carnea*; *E.e.* 'W.T. Rackliff' flowers March-April — it has a neat compact habit suitable for the raised bed, deep green foliage and pure white flowers. *Erica cinerea* 'Pink Ice' flowers June-September and the flowers continue for a long time. Its compact habit makes it a good plant for a raised bed. *E.c.* 'C.D. Eason' has glowing reddish pink flowers which continue from July to September, a most reliable variety. *Erica vagans* 'Mrs D.F. Maxwell' August to October flowering, is an old variety but still one of the best. It can always be relied upon. The flowers are cerise pink clustered thickly on long spikes. A must for all heath gardens. Other shrubs for the peat garden are:

CLETHRA ALNIFOLIA, the sweet pepper bush, which grows to about 5 feet and spreads by suckers, so it needs space and is for ground level beds only. It has clusters of small white flowers in August and is grown chiefly for its fragrance. It needs no pruning.

PERNETTYA MUCRONATA This is an evergreen shrub growing to about 2 feet. It bears many small white flowers in May-June but its main beauty is in the large rounded berries like marbles in colours of white and pink through to deep mulberry colour. To ensure cross-pollination of the flowers for the berries which follow, at least two bushes should be planted. It is attractive in a raised bed if there is sufficient room for two plants. No pruning is required.

RHODODENDRONS While rhododendrons can be left without any pruning they give a better performance over the years if dead flower heads are cut off to prevent seeding. It is therefore better to choose varieties where the flower heads can be reached with ease. The dwarf varieties mentioned below may be grown and cared for in a raised bed.

R.IMPEDITUM is an alpine species which only grows 9 in. but spreads slowly. It has mauve flowers in April-May. *R.russatum*, which grows 2½ feet, has a compact habit with violet coloured flowers in May. *R.praecox* is 3 feet with translucent pink flowers in February-March. It can be caught by frost but is particularly lovely. *R.* 'Blue Diamond' grows to 5 feet and is fairly broad. It has very small leaves and soft blue flowers in April-May. It is one of the best of the dwarf blue-flowered group.

AZALEAS are now listed under rhododendrons. The evergreen Japanese dwarf type known as 'Kurume' are very attractive and the following are known to flower well. All are suitable for a raised peat bed. 'Hinomayo', with clear pink flowers is one of the most reliable for flowering and can grow to 3 feet. 'Hinodegiri' has bright crimson flowers and a height of 2 feet. 'Hatsugiri' has crimson purple flowers and 'Kirin' pale and deep rose shaded flowers. Like the rhododendrons these plants are better for having their old flowers removed, but can still give pleasure if this is impossible.

5 Flowers

In past years it was customary to divide the garden into hard and fast sections, and to confine certain types of plants to each section. There was the shrub border containing conifer, flowering and non-flowering shrubs; all herbaceous plants were confined to the herbaceous border, and similarly, there was the rose garden, the annual border etc. In recent years the keen home gardener has learnt the value of the mixed border in which favourite plants may be grown together provided the planting is well planned and not overcrowded.

The choice of planting depends on the amount of space available. Certainly some shrubs have a place in the border; they give warmth, shelter and varied shapes, attractive in winter as well as summer. With the shrubs may be planted perennials, annuals, bulbs, and even some alpines at the edge of the border. For some people bright colours are essential, whilst others prefer softer tones, choosing plants for their garden as though painting a picture, and there are many plants to choose from.

The mixed border brings pleasant surprises: an opening bud of the shrub *Viburnum farreri (fragrans)* with its sweet scent on a sunny day in February; then there is the first crocus; or the scent of daphne, or a few winter pansies to be seen. All these long before the perennials come into flower, or before annuals are even sown!

Flower Beds

To grow so many lovely and interesting plants may be a difficulty when the bed or border can only be 2 foot wide for comfortable working within reach. A great deal depends on the gardener's ability to bend and stretch. If a wider border is needed a path can be made down the middle, the shrubs and taller plants being planted in the back half, with the shorter plants and dwarf shrubs in the front half.

When choosing the site for new beds or borders it is advisable to select a position that will receive as much sun as possible. Many plants will grow in shade, but are not so likely to produce flowers. Island beds are much in favour, and they are very attractive, but if set in grass, there is the problem of mowing round them — and, more difficult, edges to cut. Island beds set in paving cause no such difficulty, for they are approachable from all angles and so can be 4 feet wide, with a 2 foot reach from either side. With a mixed border adequate space must always be left for shrubs to make development.

The perennial plants which are chosen should be those which are self-supporting and need no staking, also those that do not need lifting, dividing and replanting every second or third year. Michaelmas daisies are of the latter group and if dividing is not done regularly, the flowers deteriorate and there is more likelihood of mildew. Such plants are not included in this chapter.

If the garden is being altered a little at a time, plants may already be in the border which need staking, and must remain there until such time as replanting may be done. For such cases plant supports may be used. These are metal frames mainly circular in shape from 15 in. in diameter upwards. There are crossing bars within the frame which stands on metal legs; these legs are pushed into the ground over the newly emerging shoots of the plant. The shoots grow up in the squares of the frame and are thus supported. Another method of supporting plants is by closer planting than normally advocated, so that plants support one another, especially if there are some sturdy ones growing among them. This is quite suitable for a small sheltered garden.

If the gardener can manage the job, the border will respond to a mulching of garden compost or peat, and certainly a feed in the spring is necessary when plants are to be in the ground for several years. 'Growmore', fertiliser is easy and clean to handle, being granular; used at 2 oz. to the square yard in March-April it will help growth considerably. On the whole perennials are not very suitable for the raised bed, except for alpines of course which come in another category.

Choice of Plants

Well intentioned friends will often give clumps of plants which have become too large for their own garden; these plants are too demanding in labour and only become a menace. It is better to buy a few choice plants which can stay put for years without much attention, need no staking and are sturdy enough to stand up to wind and rain of their own accord. The following pages contain some suggestions of plants that can be planted with confidence by those people who have physical difficulties.

ACANTHUS MOLLIS and A.SPINOSUS are similar plants, mollis having soft leaves and spinosus prickly ones. Both species stand up boldly with strong spikes of flowers arising from the beautifully shaped dark evergreen leaves. Their architectural form makes a focal point in the garden. They like a sunny position and a well-drained soil. Though height is 3-4 feet no staking is needed.

ANAPHALIS TRIPLINERVIS These silver foliaged plants are useful as a foil for gayer colours. They bear white flowers which are ever-lasting. They like full sun and are useful at the edge of a bed or border. They are easy to grow and reach a height of 12 in.

ANEMONE JAPONICA The Japanese anemone flowers in late summer and into autumn, and is invaluable in the garden. It may take a little while to settle down, but thereafter gives flowers year after year and seems to thrive on neglect. The foliage is coarse in texture but attractively lobed, and the saucer shaped flowers of pink or white are borne on two and a half foot stems. This plant needs no staking and once planted resents disturbance. There are several named varieties. Planting distance is 12 in.

AQUILEGIA or 'Columbine', an attractive plant 6-12 in. high according to variety, the soft leaves are similar to maidenhair fern in appearance. The bi-coloured flowers have spurs to the petals, which gives them an airy grace. No staking is required. It is not a long-lived plant, but sets seed easily. Aquilegias need moisture but will grow and flower in partial shade. A perennial plant which would be suitable for a raised bed.

ARTEMISIA ABSINTHUM 'Lambrook Silver' is grown for its beautiful silver foliage. The common name is 'Wormwood'. Both the height and spread of one plant is 3 feet. It must have well drained soil.

BERGENIA called 'Elephant Ears' because of the large leathery leaves persistent through the winter. Large trusses of pink or red flowers appear in March-April. It is a handsome plant, easy to grow happy in the driest conditions or deep shade. *B.cordifolia* has heart-shaped leaves. The variety 'Ballawley hybrid' bears the largest trusses of flowers — rose-red and set in handsome leaves. It is a very well worthwhile plant, height about 14 in, spread about 24 in. If it is possible it is better to remove dead flower heads; this can be done with the 'Baronet' long-armed cutter.

CAMPANULA One of the easiest campanulas to grow is *C.persicifolia* 'Telham Beauty'. It is a beautiful, rather delicate looking herbaceous plant, that is easily grown from seed. It has slender 2 foot stems bearing blue saucer-shaped flowers. It needs no staking, will grow and bloom in sun or shade, and is quite happy to be left alone.

CHRYSANTHEMUM MAXIMUM is the 'Shasta Daisy', coarse in growth as well as rampant. There is now a good variety 'Little Silver Princess' growing to about 18 in, and flowering June-August. It is easily grown from seed sown out of doors, and needs no staking.

DIANTHUS, garden pinks are a great favourite; they need a light well drained soil in full sun, and look well in the front of the border, both for their flowers in summer and the silver leaves in winter. The *allwoodii* type are deservedly popular. They can be grown in a raised bed and do particularly well between tyres when a raised bed is being made from these.

DICENTRA SPECTABILIS, known as 'Bleeding Heart' or 'Dutchman's Breeches', has pendant pink and white flowers on arching stems while the leaves are fern-like. It flowers in April-June in either sun or shade, and needs reasonable moisture. The plant dies down after flowering.

DORONICUM, the 'Leopards Bane', has bright yellow daisy-like flowers which appear usually in profusion, in early April; the plant forms low-growing clumps. Doronicum will grow in most soils and in sun or shade. One of the best varieties is 'Harpur Crewe'. It is worth having for its early flowers.

ECHINOPS RITRO is the blue globe thistle. If the variety 'Veitch's Blue' is chosen (which grows to 2½ feet) no staking is required. The leaves are grey-green and thistle like. It is of value in the border for its architectural beauty.

ERYNGIUM is the prickly sea-holly and a most handsome plant. It likes full sun and well drained soil (the wild form grows on sand dunes). It needs no staking and dislikes disturbance. It is excellent for floral arrangements and for drying. The variety *E.amethystinum* grows to 2 feet and has teazle-like heads of amethyst blue.

EUPHORBIA has become more popular of recent years. The flowers are inconspicuous, but they are surrounded by bright yellow-green bracts in spring. One of the easiest to grow which does not ramp too much is *E.polychroma (epithymoides)*. It is an attractive sight in spring, growing to 18 in. It is a trouble free plant and well worth having. *E.griffithii* is much taller but does not need staking; the bracts of this species are bright red and make a good show in early summer. It does spread over the years, so it is not advisable to grow it in a small garden.

GERANIUMS The cranesbill is a hardy perennial. Some geraniums are useful for ground cover, while many can be used in borders. The smaller species go on flowering for a long time. *G.renardii* has silvery leaves and white flowers. *G.endressii* 'Rose Clair' continues to bloom throughout the summer. Both prefer partial shade. Those geraniums grown in greenhouses and bedded out are in fact pelargoniums.

HELLEBORUS The 'Christmas Rose' is well known, if only on Christmas cards; this is *Helleborus niger*, it needs moist condi-

Raised bed at the Royal Horticultural Society's garden, the edge of this bed is wide enough to sit *n. Sink gardens beyond.*

Raised bed at the Royal Horticultural Society's garden. Built higher at one end to compensate for *ifference in gradient.*

3   above, *Raised bed made of peat blocks showing effect of planting between blocks.*

4   opposite top, *Close-up of peat blocks showing manner of building.*

5   opposite bottom, *Raised bed made of tyres, seen 18 months after planting. Ivies, sedums, dwarf cytisus and aubretia used for interplanting.*

6   above, *Glazed sink covered with attractively planted Hypertufa, in the Royal Horticultural Society's garden for disabled people at Wisley.*

7   opposite top, *Plant container made from wheel with tyre. Can be raised to the required height.*

8   opposite bottom, *The Royal Horticultural Society's garden for disabled people at Wisley incorporates many features to give assistance to differing handicaps.*

9   above, *A garden outside a church hall in London for the use of able and disabled people of the Pinwheel Club, affiliated to the Greater London Association for the Disabled.*

10   below, *An elderly person's balcony garden put to full use for growing plants.*

11   right, *Raised pool at the demonstration garden for disabled people in Battersea Park, London.*

2 opposite top, *A raised bed, designed for an ambulant person who is unable to bend, in the garden at Battersea Park.*

3 opposite bottom, *Further types of raised beds made of pre-cast walling stone.*

4 above, *Sitting on an inverted easi-kneeler stool to work at a raised bed using mini-tools.*

15   above, *Garden for handicapped children in Battersea Park.*

16   opposite top, *Members of the gardening club of the Royal Hospital & Home for Incurables, enjoying a meeting and gardening demonstration in the garden at Battersea Park.*

17   opposite bottom, *Useful tools. From left to right: mini-hoe and mini-cultivator (Wolf); the Baronet weeder and Baronet cut-and-hold flower gatherer (Wright); a three-foot handle fork (Wilkinson); the push-pull weeder and a cultivator (Wolf).*

18   above, *Using the 'Anita Grab' for picking up rubbish without bending.*

19   opposite top, Tulipa tarda, *which can be left in the ground from year to year. Yellow flowers tipped white; very bright in spring.*

20   opposite bottom, *The day-lily,* Hemerocallis X 'Golden Chimes', *which does not grow too large.*

21 left, *A good garden shrub which needs little or no pruning is* Potentilla X 'Elizabeth' *which has pale yellow flowers over a long period.*

22 below, Hypericum calycinum *is an easy-to-grow ground cover plant.*

23 opposite top *The dwarf thyme* T. serpyllum '*Pink Chintz*' *makes attractive ground cover for smaller areas.*

24 opposite bottom, Euphorbia epithymoides (polychroma) *is bright yellow-green in spring and well worth having.*

25 *Looking down on* Sedum spectabile *beside a path. It has proved an attraction for the small tortoiseshell butterfly.*

tions and likes shade so can be grown amongst shrubs.

H.ORIENTALIS is often known as the 'Lenten Rose'. The flowers vary in colour from greenish white through pink to dark purple. It likes peat when planted, and at least partial shade. Left alone the Lenten Rose will gradually form good clumps and give flowers very early in the year; it is best left undisturbed. While most hellebores prefer a rich soil with lime in it, *H.corsicus* thrives quite happily in most conditions if moved when young. It grows to 2½ feet, and maintains its sculptured leathery green leaves throughout the year. Pale apple-green flowers appear in January-February and persist through March. It is attractive all the year round, needs no staking and resents disturbance, it will appreciate a mulching if this is possible. *H.foetidus* is similar in height, with finely divided dark leaves and smaller flowers. It is not quite so attractive but is a good plant for full shade.

HEMEROCALLIS is the 'Day Lily', so called as individual flowers only last one day, but the flowers are prolific and give a continuous display. It is another very good garden plant but clumps might become rather large for the small garden. Hemerocallis is adaptable to a wide range of soils, 'heavy' or 'light', wet or dry, the plants will still flourish and bloom. They need no staking, resent disturbance, and are generally considered trouble free. The leaves are rush-like and grow to 2-3 feet depending on variety. Flower colours range from pale yellow to dark red; for example, 'Black Magic' deep mahogany, 'Whichford' pale primrose, and 'Golden Chimes' dwarf in habit.

HEUCHERA or 'Coral bells'. These plants form flat rosettes of dark leaves at ground level from which grow thin wiry stems bearing coral, deep pink, or pale pink flowers. They are plants which do well at the front of the border, but are not happy in heavy clay where they tend to die. If on a light soil in sun or partial shade they thrive and can be left undisturbed. Varieties are 'Coral Cloud' and 'Red Spangles.'

HOSTA or 'Plantain Lily'. These plants are grown mainly for their bold and beautiful leaves, they grow best in partial shade. Some varieties have heart-shaped leaves 1½ feet in length. They grow slowly making a large clump and need mulching with leaf-mould if possible. The variegated leaved

variety 'Thomas Hogg' is one of the best. The plants do bear
racemes of lilac coloured flowers but these are considered
secondary to the leaves.

KNIPHOFIA or 'Red Hot Poker'. A group of these plants
makes a splendid focal point in the garden; there are several
species and very many varieties, so there is enough choice as
to height and colour to suit the proportions of most gardens.
When newly planted they need a little protection for the first
winter only till they are well established. The flower spikes of
some reach 5 feet while others only 20 ins. 'Royal Standard'
is the old variety with rather coarse growth; in 'Bees Sunset'
the whole 'poker' is brilliant flame colour; while *K.galpinii* is
a dainty species with grass-like leaves and the flower spike
less than 20 in. long. These plants need a sunny position if
possible; they will grow in most soils provided it is well
drained, particularly in winter. Cheerful and bright, they can
be left undisturbed for years.

L.NUMMULARIA is the well-known 'Creeping Jenny' which can
prove much too invasive and difficult to control, but *L.punctata*,
the yellow loosestrife, will grow almost anywhere, and is useful
in places where little else will grow, not minding complete
shade. Where other plants grow well do not plant this one as it
might take over.

LYTHRUM VIRGATUM 'Rose Queen' is a relative of the pru-
ple loosestrife which grows by rivers, but it is quite happy in
garden soils. It looks well by a pool. 'Rose Queen' grows to 3
feet and will not need staking if a group of plants is closely
planted.

PAEONY The cottage garden paeony is the big double red
one, but now there are many beautiful varieties, single and
double, with a range of colours. They are fine plants and the
leaves are attractive when the flowers are over. Once planted
they resent disturbance and may be left without moving for
as long as 50 years (for the first few years after planting flowers will be few). Plants grow in sun or dappled shade. They
do require a rich well-drained soil, and if leaf-mould or garden compost can be given as a top dressing they will much
appreciate it. The variety 'Sarah Bernhardt' has large pale
pink flowers; 'Felix Crousse' carmine red, 'Festiva maxima'
white flecked crimson.

POLYGONUM Some species of this plant grow too strongly and are difficult to control, but *P.affine* 'Donald Lowndes' has compact growth with bright red flower spikes of six ins. It will grow in sun or shade and is suitable for a raised bed.

PRIMULA DENTICULATA is the 'drumstick primula' which will grow in a border and is most attractive in a raised bed. This primula will grow in sun or shade, but is better in shade if the soil is sandy or gravelly. It flowers March-April and the colours range from white through mauve to deep purple.

PULMONARIA, the lungwort, is a delightful spring-flowering plant for shaded places. Some species have attractive spotted leaves such as *P.saccharata* whose flowers are pink in bud turning blue as they open. The leaves die down in mid-summer. This plant needs plenty of moisture in early spring; average height is 1 foot.

SEDUM This is a large genus and the bigger type grown in the border is known as 'Ice plant'. These sedums have thick fleshy leaves in rosettes. In autumn flat heads of pink flowers are borne on stems 1 foot long. These flowers are worth growing as they are very attractive to butterflies. Plants grow best in the sun. Varieties include 'Autumn Joy' and 'Ruby Glow'.

SOLIDAGO, the golden rod, is an old favourite, and in the past plants were tall and of loose growth. Newer varieties are more robust and do not need staking. These plants do well in cool shade. Varieties include 'Cloth of Gold' at 18 in., 'Goldenmosa', 2½ feet and 'Golden Wings' 2½ feet.

TRADESCANTIA is the spiderwort or 'Wandering Jew' which will grow almost anywhere in sun or shade. The leaves are rush-like but short and the three-petalled flowers arise down in the centre of the clump continuously from June to September. It is not a showy plant but is easy to grow. Good varieties are 'Taplow Crimson' and 'Purple Dome'.

Annuals

There are two main groups of annuals, hardy and half-hardy; the former can be sown directly into the flower border or raised bed in March-April. Half-hardy annuals have the seed sown in boxes, pricked out into more boxes to give them room to develop (both these jobs may be done sitting down), then planted out in mid-May or June. These half-hardy annuals are usually known as 'bedding plants' and can be bought ready for planting if the gardener cannot raise them himself. Buying bedding plants is probably worthwhile for a window box, raised bed or containers, but would prove expensive for a large area as when the plants only last one season.

Sowing seed of hardy annuals 'in situ' is useful for filling odd gaps in a border or having lovely bursts of colour in a raised bed. The soil needs to be raked reasonably fine in preparation; in a raised bed the Wolf mini-rake is useful for this. Then the area to be sown is demarcated by 'drawing' the outline with a trickle of sand. An irregularly shaped outline looks more natural, each type of plant having its own area. Within the area straight drills are drawn with a sharp-pointed stick, the stick being of a length to suit the person using it, and longer for the border, shorter for a raised bed. Drills should be about 4-6 in. apart depending on the height of the plant being sown; when germinated the seedlings will be in rows and so distinguished from any weed seedlings. When fully grown there will be no sign of straight rows, but just an irregularly shaped patch of flowers.

The choice of annuals is legion as any good catalogue will show. The majority of them like the sun, but there are some that will bloom well in shade. Many annuals need to be dead-headed, to give continuous bloom. This can be an enjoyable task sitting at a raised bed, provided one hand is strong enough to use clippers or the useful one-handed shears, but at ground level this can prove a difficult task, and if not dead-headed many annuals seed and die, whereas with attention they go on flowering the whole season. The 'Baronet' cut-and-hold flower gatherer is useful for this as it is long-handled and can be used from a sitting position, or when standing saves bending.

When choosing annuals for a raised bed, care should be taken not to choose those that grow too tall, otherwise their beauty is missed by the sitting gardener. Many catalogues now show dwarf varieties of old favourites.

Naturalising Annuals Some gardeners who have large spaces

to fill, allow their hardy annuals to seed themselves year after year; they certainly give quite a colourful display the first year of seeding, but after that the flowers tend to become smaller. Even so this is better than an area of weeds. The Forget-me-not, a biennial, will have smaller flowers if it naturalises itself, and those of deep blue shades will return to the typical pale blue, but they make sheets of colour and are not to be despised. Cornflowers seed themselves, and bird-watchers will enjoy watching goldfinches feeding on the seed heads. Nigella or 'Love-in-the-mist' is yet another that will seed. The English marigold seeds itself everywhere, but tends to have too much foliage with a diminishing size of flowers over the years. Certainly natural seeding with smaller flowers fills up a space that cannot otherwise be managed, and brings many interesting seed-eating birds as well. Though a biennial and not annual, the foxglove regenerates itself and helps to fill odd spaces, especially shady ones.

Much information may be gained from catalogues about annuals, but the following are worth particular mention as having been grown by gardeners with varying physical handicaps.

ALYSSUM or 'Little Dorrit' can be sown in a greenhouse February-March, or in the open ground April-May. No dead-heading is needed. As well as the white form there are mauve varieties.

CALLISTEPHUS, China aster, is an old favourite. Treatment is the same as for 'Little Dorrit'. There are now many wilt-resistant varieties, and dwarf ones suitable for raised beds and containers such as Sutton's 'Dwarf Queen', 8 in. or 'Pepite' 12 in.

CORNFLOWER Both blue and mixed colours are attractive. The dwarf forms now available are much neater and do not need any support. The seeds of cornflower may be sown out-of-doors in September and the seedlings withstand the winter to give early flowers.

DIMORPHOTHECA 'Star of the Veld'. Seed can be bought in a mixture of lovely colours; sown in April the plants will give a continuous display throughout the summer, provided they are in a sunny spot.

TAGETES, French marigold. Seeds are best started in a

greenhouse, or plants bought. The value of these plants is that they need no dead-heading but continue to bloom throughout the summer, they also flower well in shade, and are not spoilt by a wet season. This a good plant for the gardener who is unable to give much attention to his plants. 'Spanish Brocade' is one good variety out of many.

IMPATIENS, 'Busy Lizzie' is well known as an indoor plant but there are now relatives for outdoor planting. It is definitely half-hardy and seed must be sown in a greenhouse or plants bought. Sutton's variety 'Minette mixed' grows flat along the surface of the soil, spreading out in carpets of colour. It flowers well in partial shade, seems indifferent to wet seasons and keeps brilliant colour without dead-heading, making a good show in a raised bed.

LEPTOSIPHON 'Star Dust' can be sown in the open ground and is ideal for miniature gardens or raised beds. It is very dwarf and the fine green foliage is studded with tiny flowers in colours ranging from cream to orange and red.

NIGELLA, Love-in-the-mist, can be sown in the open in September. The delicate blue flowers come in spring and are not very long-lasting, but the attractive seed heads are much used in flower arrangements.

PETUNIAS can look really exotic; they are half-hardy and cannot be sown in the open. In spite of their frail appearance they will both stand up to rain and bloom in the shade. They do give better results when dead-headed, but will continue to flower without.

RUDBECKIA, 'Irish Eyes', is an annual variety of an old favourite. It has yellow petals and a green centre. The seed can be sown May-June for flowering the following year. They are bold plants with stiff erect stems of 18 in. No staking is required, and they stand up to all weathers. They are excellent for cutting and will bloom up until November if there are no bad frosts.

ZINNIA, Peter Pan varieties are only 10 in. high, but have full-sized flowers. Seed is sown in the greenhouse, one seed per pot, then planted out in June. Zinnias are grown this way as they resent disturbance. These small ones do well in a raised bed.

Bulbs Corms and Tubers

When bulbs are mentioned thoughts immediately turn to spring; to snowdrops and crocuses, followed by daffodils then tulips, after which bulbs are usually forgotten. There are however many bulbs and corms for summer and autumn, which can stay in the ground naturalising themselves.

This section will deal with bulbs, corms and tubers for all seasons, omitting gladiolus and dahlias as these need staking, lifting at the end of the season and storing in winter, all of which means a great deal of work, which cannot always be undertaken. Once planted, bulbs and corms can give joy for many years. Soil and water requirements may differ for the various types, but the majority need planting at three times their own depth, that is, to have twice their own depth of soil above them, except for a few and notes will be given on these.

Spring bulbs

CHIONODOXA 'Glory of the Snow', a delightful name for the star shaped flower with a white centre. Height about 6 in. These bulbs prefer to flower in full sun; they are planted in autumn in groups.

CROCUS This flower needs no description, but it is usually the 'Dutch' crocus in colours of purple white and yellow that are grown. These do not set seed but have offsets which can be divided if wished. The crocus species however are fascinating to grow; they vary in colour (with many combinations) in size, and to some extent shape, while most of them seed themselves. By planting corms of these, in a few years they will have increased. A crocus species collection in a raised bed is ideal; the corms will have perfect drainage, and if the summers are hot, they will revel in it.

There are many species listed in catalogues, some with varieties. The *C.chrysanthus* 'Goldilocks' is deep yellow with a rich purple base; *C.c.* 'Moonlight' pale sulphur to cream; *C.c.* 'Zwanenburg' bronze; and *C.tomasinianus* which will flower as early as January, often showing through the snow, colour varying from pale silvery mauve to quite a deep colour. This species seeds very freely indeed, and will spring up all over the garden. It is a tough little corm and a crocus no garden

71

should be without. It is not suitable for a raised bed, however, as it might 'take over' and the leaves would have to die before any further planting could be done. *C.biflorus* 'Weldenii' is another crocus that is free flowering, coloured white and pale blue. *C.sieberi* is a medium sized crocus and one of the most beautiful, deep mauve with orange-yellow throat *C.susianus* is the 'Cloth of Gold' crocus, golden yellow with bronze feathering on the outside.

HARDY CYCLAMEN These tiny plants are very beautiful, like our indoor cyclamen in miniature. They prefer some shade and will thrive in most soils including chalky ones. They dislike any water-logging. A spring flowering one is *C.coum*, the strong pink flowers appearing January-March. They can be grown in a raised bed provided they have plenty of shade from other plants. They will seed themselves.

ERANTHIS HYEMALIS is the winter aconite. This plant with cup shaped flowers of brightest yellow appears very early in the year. It grows from a tuber and left alone it gradually spreads. It is planted late summer in sun or shade, and needs plenty of moisture in the spring when it is making growth.

LEUCOJUM VERNUM is the spring snowflake, white in colour as the name suggests. The snowflake has a much more rounded flower than the snowdrop, and the plant grows taller. It likes a cool moist soil and is tolerant of lime. It flowers in March and flowers increase after it has become established.

MUSCARI, the grape hyacinth. This small bulb bearing blue flowers is well known and worth growing. It is a free flowering bulb which also propagates itself, and when it becomes too thick may need dividing. It is lime tolerant and prefers being planted in full sun. There are several varieties from pale to deep blue.

NARCISSI This is a very large genus that cannot be dealt with in this book except for one or two special varieties. For ground level and raised beds there are some delightful small varieties. 'February Gold' grows to 10 in., the whole of the flower being deep yellow and the perianth slightly reversed. In the north it does not bloom until March. 'Peeping Tom' is very similar but flowers a month later. Both varieties remain in flower three to four weeks, giving much pleasure. Miniature daffodils and narcissi are particularly effective in a raised bed. *N.bulbicodium*, the hoop petticoat narcissi grows to 6 in. and has a circular shaped trumpet, hence its name; it flowers in March-April. *N.triandrus 'albus'* is the 'Angels tears'; it has a reflexed perianth and two to three flowers on a 6 in. stem, flowering in April. Narcissi are also very useful for naturalising.

ORNITHOGALUM UMBELLATUM is the 'Star of Bethlehem' which has a truss of white flowers with green outer stripes. The flowers are borne on short stalks and bloom in April-May. This plant propagates itself by offsets and can spread quite rapidly, so it is not suitable for a raised bed. It looks very well among shrubs.

SCILLA The squill is closely related to the chionodoxa and is a hardy bulb. Its flowers growing to about 6 in., there are three to four stems per bulb, and each stem bears three bell shaped flowers which are blue. It can be planted in sun or shade. *S.sibirica* is very well known, it is a brilliant blue and well worth having. *S.tubergeniana* is a very pale blue with a deeper blue stripe on the outside; it is very lovely and flowers early in January — the delicate colour shows up well on a dull day. Both these species would look well in a raised bed.

TULIP Only the tulip species will be mentioned here, as unlike the Darwins, Mayflowering etc., these species may be left in the ground undisturbed to give colour for several years. Species tulips are short in the stem so are unlikely to be broken of suffer wind damage. Many have brilliant colours. Catalogues give a full list but the following are a few to brighten the front of a border or plant in a raised bed.

T.eichleri is flame red and grows to a height of 10 in., flowering at the end of April. *T.greigii* and its hybrids have beautifully marked and mottled leaves. A mixture of these hybrids makes a most colourful display in April. *T.praestans* 'Fusilier' bears three orange-scarlet flowers to a stem. None of these tulips should be planted before October; they like a sunny position in well drained soil and appreciate a dressing of lime.

Summer Bulbs

ALLIUMS The onion is an allium, but of those listed below very few have an onion smell unless definitely bruised. The following species have well coloured flowers and are quite hardy and easy to grow, preferring a sunny situation. *A.moly* is 10 in. high and has yellow blooms in June. *A.oreophilum* grows to 5 feet and has red flowers in June. *A.ursinum* is the wild ramsones and should not be grown; it is far too invasive and will get out of control, also on a warm day, without being touched it will smell of garlic.

CAMASSIA These are not very showy plants, yet they have their own beauty. The flowers are star shaped, and are in colours of white, cream and mauvish-blue. They can be very useful in a mixed flower border, being quite hardy and easy to grow. They like moisture and are bulbs that will stand up to wet winters, a useful plant for moist ground. They set seed and can be propagated this way. *C.cusickii*, 2½ feet, has blue star shaped flowers in June-July. *C.leichtlinii* grows to 3 feet, and has creamy white flowers. but colour can be variable. It flowers in June.

CYCLAMEN NEAPOLITANUM This is the most well known of the hardy cyclamen. The flowers appear in August just before the leaves; there are pink and white varieties. These plants prefer some shade and will grow at the base of trees. The roots arise on the *top* of the tuber so the smooth rounded part is placed facing downward when planting; the shoot also arises from the top. The leaves are very beautifully marked green and silver, no two plants exactly alike, the leaves persisting throughout the winter. Cyclamen seed themselves, and as the seed sets the stem curls back like a watchspring. They will grow in a raised bed if it is shaded for part of the day.

LEUCOJUM AESTIVUM This is the summer snowflake. It is found growing wild on river banks and in wet areas. It grows to about 2 feet, and likes conditions the same as for the spring snowflake.

LILIUMS The growing of lilies is a subject on its own, but many lilies, once planted, object to being moved which makes them suitable for a permanent planting. They like their roots in the shade and heads in the sun, and will often grow well among shrubs. They do need mulching, and staking when necessary is often wire-netting placed round the whole clump. One of the easier species to grow is *L.regale* which can be raised from seed and is known to flower in its second or third year; it is lime tolerant, but it can grow to 5 feet and needs support.

Autumn Bulbs

COLCHICUMS, or meadow saffron, are often called 'autumn crocus' but the latter belong to a different family. Colchicums grow from a tuber and not a corm. The flowers are large; appearing before the leaves they look very frail and rather naked. The tubers are planted in July-August in a moist area. The leaves which develop later are rather large. *C.autumnale* has several varieties including pink and white. *C.speciosum* which is considered the best has violet-mauve flowers.

AUTUMN CROCUS, the true autumn crocus, is similar to the species of the spring ones; corms need to be planted as soon as they are available, that is about July. *C.speciosus* is deep violet-blue, a good colour, and it sets seed freely. It would look well in a raised bed or border that can be seen from the house as it will flower late in the year.

SCHIZOSTYLIS COCCINEA is the 'Kaffir Lily' and is not strictly a bulb, but a swollen rhizome; the flowers are star-like and red or pink; the flower stem grows to about 2 feet. As these plants flower late in the autumn they need a warm sunny position. There are two varieties usually available, 'Mrs Hegarty' rose-pink and 'Viscountess Byng' pale shell pink. In the north this bulb needs the shelter of a frame or greenhouse.

STERNBERGIA LUTEA Once a gardener takes an interest in bulbs, this one should not be forgotten. It is not always easy to grow but does make a challenge to the keen grower. As it needs very well drained soil it could be grown in a raised bed. The flowers are golden yellow, rather like a crocus in shape; leaves and flowers come together. It is planted 6 in. deep in August, and must be left undisturbed. It gives the best flowers after a really hot summer.

Rock Plants

The word 'alpines' has become a general name for plants that are grown in rock gardens, but such plants do not all come from the alps. Rock plants including the true alpines come from a wide variety of habitats; however they all have one thing in common, the need for perfect drainage. For this the raised bed is ideal, because sufficient drainage may be put in the bottom of the bed, and the right compost for the plants to grow in. Alpines or rock plants need plenty of water during the growing season, but it should be able to drain away freely and *never* accumulate in the compost. If varying composts are needed e.g. an area for lime-hating plants a cross wall may be built into the raised bed, dividing it into separate areas for plants with differing soil needs.

Most rock plants are small, some are very tiny indeed, and when these plants are grown in a raised bed, not only can they be given the right conditions, but are also brought up nearer to eye level so that their fine beauty can be fully appreciated.

A sink garden (see chapter 2) makes a delightful container for rock plants, and they look particularly attractive if a dwarf conifer is included. The bushy types of plants such as aubretias, arabis, helianthemum (rock rose) may be grown in a dry wall; these plants though beautiful tend to get in the way when overhanging a raised bed. For anyone either with or without a disability, a rock garden can be a difficult place to work in. Keeping it weeded and cared for without damaging very small plants is not easy; a container or raised bed is much more convenient. This should be sited in an open position with as much sunlight as possible; there are rock plants which prefer shade, or partial shade but they are in the minority.

For a bed 2 feet in depth, 9 in. of drainage is sufficient using broken pots, stones, etc., over this is placed material which will prevent the compost from being washed away through the drainage. Turves placed grass downward are the best, but if unavailable coarse peat will do. The compost is then put on the top to a depth of 12-15 in. Compost bought especially for the purpose can prove very expensive; it is surprising the amount that is needed even in a bed 4 feet by 4 feet. Used John Innes compost with a little more sharp sand added is excellent, or a compost may be made from garden soil, provided it is not of a sticky clay consistency or has no pernicious weeds in it like convolvulus, dandelion, ground elder etc. Two parts of garden soil may be used with one part fine moss peat and one part sharp sand. If the soil is on the 'heavy' side a little fine washed pea gravel may be added to assist drainage. The soil needs to be lightly firmed and allowed to settle, preferably through a fall of rain, before planting. The soil will most likely sink, then more soil may be added. It is surprising how much the soil subsides in a raised bed over a few years, some people grow annuals the first year, thus avoiding disapointment in the permanent planting.

Choice of Plants

The following list of plants has been chosen with the handicapped person in mind. These plants are easy to grow and are recommended to start with; once these plants have been grown successfully it will be a short step to try others. Libraries have many books on the subject, while catalogues give much information; but before reading how to grow the more difficult plants, the easy ones should be attempted. Practical experience in the garden will not only give great joy, but also teach the gardener what the various plants need to grow and to flourish.

Rock plants may also be grown in a bed at ground level, this may be preferable for people who find it easier to work in a sitting position on the ground, moving from one cushion to another.

ACHILLEA 'King Edward' is a mat-forming plant which has flat heads of creamy-white flowers from summer through to autumn. It is propagated by cuttings or division and will flower in sun or shade.

AETHIONEMA 'Warley Rose' is a neat shrubby little plant 6 in. high. It has carmine flower heads like candytuft, which continue over a long period from May onwards if in the sun, and is propagated by cuttings.

ALYSSUM SAXATILE 'Citrinum'. The deep yellow alyssum is well known but this variety has paler flowers, and the growth is more compact; even so it is not for the raised bed, but can be used on a bank or in a dry wall. It can be easily propagated from seed.

ARABIS The white arabis, so well known, has large coarse growth but *A.blepharophylla* 'Spring Charm' is a different species with dwarf compact growth of about 6 in., and bears deep pink flowers. It is easily grown from seed and is ideal for a raised bed or for the edge of borders.

ARENARIA MONTANA This little plant grows well from seed, making green cushions with small white flowers.

ARMERIA MARITIMA is the thrift of the seaside, growing on the cliffs. There are many good garden forms with colours of deep pink and red. It grows well in a raised bed, and can also be used at the edge of a mixed border.

CAMPANULA This is a very large genus; some of the best for a raised bed are: *C.carpatica* 'Isobel' which makes a neat mound of growth with blue flowers 2 in. across, and is easy to grow; *C.hallii*, an attractive small bell of white; *C.pusilla*, very small and called the 'Fairies Thimble'. *C.pusilla* does spread by underground runners but is easily controllable. *C.portensclagiana* should be avoided at all costs, it is beautiful but ramps everywhere, uplifting paving slabs, and the more it is pulled out, the more it appears elsewhere.

CHRYSANTHEMUM HARADJANII 'Prince of Wales Feather' is grown for its feathery cut-leaf of silver grey.

DIANTHUS 'Pinks' are always a great favourite. The Cheddar Pink, *D.gratianopolitanus* is easy to grow and sweetly scented. *D.deltoides* grows to 6 in. and its brilliantly coloured carmine flowers are a 'must' for a raised bed; it can also be grown in dry walls and on banks. An easy plant and once established seed can be collected for propagating.

Hebe 'Carl Teschner' is a shrubby plant with small leaves and numerous small purple flowers. Excellent for growing in the bed of a double wall, though it is not always hardy in the north.

HELIANTHEMUM, Rock Rose. This plant likes a light soil and full sun; the growth is rather too big for a raised bed unless this is large, but it is ideal for a sandy bank or a wall. Varieties include 'Wisley Pink', 'Jubilee' yellow, 'Sudbury Gem' deep bright pink.

HYPERICUM POLYPHYLLUM, an easily grown plant for a sunny bank, has small leaves and golden yellow flowers.

IBERIS is the perennial candytuft with dark green leaves and white flowers. It grows large but the variety 'Little Gem' is small and neat in habit, suitable for a raised bed.

IRIS PUMILA, the dwarf flag iris, is only 6 in. high. It has purple and yellow varieties. The rhizomes should not be planted deeply, but the tops show above the surface of the soil.

JUNIPERUS COMMUNIS 'Compressa' is the dwarf pencil-shaped juniper which grows very slowly, a beautiful little tree for raised bed sink, or trough.

PHLOX The dwarf phlox make sheets of colour; *P.subulata* and its varieties are the easiest to grow. *P.s.* 'Blue Eyes' is a good colour and *P.s.* 'Temiscaming' is a brilliant carmine red. These plants are better for a trimming over when the flowers have died; this can be done with scissors.

SALIX BOYDII is a dwarf willow which, once established, has miniature catkins in the spring.

SAXIFRAGE These plants are probably the first to come to mind when alpines are mentioned. The Kabschia group are the 'cushion saxifrages' which flower February-April. They need plenty of drainage and like a sunny position with watering in dry weather. Ideal for raised beds sinks etc. Varieties include *S.jenkinsae* pink, and *S.burseriana* 'Sulphurea' soft yellow. The mossy saxifrages like a cool situation, otherwise their leaves become scorched by the sun and the plant is ruined; a good variety is 'Ballawley Guardsman'. The London Pride is a saxifrage; it is rather large and spreads too easily for good control, but there is a neat miniature one only 5 in. high named *S.umbrosa* var. *Primuloides*.

SEDUMS make up another large group of plants, some of which grow wild in Britain. Most sedums grow easily and will survive neglect if they cannot always be attended to. *S.spathulifolium* 'Purpureum' has spoon shaped leaves which keep their purple colour in winter. *S.spathulifolium* 'Cappa blanca' has leaves of glistening silver white. *S.spurium* has prostrate growth with rosy-crimson flower heads, very easy to propagate by pieces broken off.

SEMPERVIVUMS or 'Houseleeks' are so named as they were often seen growing on the roofs of houses which indicated how little soil they need. They are particularly useful for growing in very shallow containers, such as an old pedestal bird-bath. A collection of these houseleeks make good contrasts in form and colour particularly when flowering. *S.tectorum* 'Mahogany' has both shape and colour; *S.arachnoidem* is covered with a silver webbing. These are particularly good plants to grow for the person who is able to use his her hands but little. They are not only attractive plants to grow but very interesting and well worth trying.

THYMUS DRUCEI (SERPYLLUM) The little creeping thyme of the chalk hills has many beautiful varieties in the garden, 'Pink Chintz' being a favourite. Though the leaves of this plant are small it grows rapidly and could soon cover a sink or raised bed, unless kept cut back. Leaving it to grow as it will it is ideal for a dry wall, and is excellent in the interstices of a raised peat bed, helping to bind the blocks.

Propagation

The various methods of producing young plants are known as 'plant propagation'. These methods fall into two main groups a) sexual i.e. by seed and b) vegetative, i.e. by using parts of the plant e.g. cuttings and leaves. Plant propagation is a fascinating job, which for the most part may be done sitting down. If the gardener has a greenhouse, many happy hours can be spent caring for the seedlings and rooted cuttings; the one drawback is that in his enthusiasm he can find he has far too many plants on his hands which he cannot find a home for!

To understand fully all the different methods of propagating, a good book needs to be consulted; here only seed sowing and stem cuttings are discussed.

Seed sowing, and pricking out Seed is sown in either plastic trays or pots, and if a loamless compost is used it will prove light to hold and clean to handle. Some people prefer the John Innes compost (referred to as 'JI') which is a mixture of loam, peat and sand with the addition of fertiliser. J.I. is available at many garden centres and garden shops, but to be sure that its composition is correct as well as the method of making it, it is advisable to buy only that which has the label on the bag with the words 'John Innes Manufacturing Association'.

With loamless composts no firming is needed, only a levelling off; but a certain amount of firming is needed with J.I. compost. Seeds need to be sown very thinly; if hands are spastic this can be difficult, so a template may be made with holes at fairly close intervals into which the seed is dropped. Once germinated the seedlings start to grow, but cannot develop without more space, so they must then be 'pricked out' into another box with about 1 in. between each seedling. A template may also be made for this to mark the position of the holes. The seedlings are usually ready for pricking out when the first true leaves appear; this means they are still very tiny and difficult to pick up. The small plants and soil may be loosened with an old table fork then each seedling can be picked up with the small fork that is supplied with a box of dates. This is a most useful tool for small seedlings as the 'fork' part slips easily underneath the leaves of the seedling which can then be lifted and dropped into the new hole without causing any damage to the very young growth, and

Using a date fork for lifting seedling and a thick-handled dibber for weak hands

also does not give rise to exasperation on the part of the gardener.

Holes to receive the seedlings are made with a dibber; this is usually made by sharpening a piece of wood to a blunted point, or dibbers may be bought. In either case it can be difficult for arthritic hands to grip a dibber but if the top part is inserted into a larger squared piece of wood, it is much easier to hold.

Cuttings Taking cuttings is fascinating, and records may be kept when experimenting with different methods. With most plants the young growth chosen is cut below a node (joint) and put into a sandy compost and kept in a close atmosphere until roots have formed. Tops of clear plastic to go over the trays or pots can be bought for this purpose. The main difficulty for some people is to take cuttings with one hand only. If, say, a pelargonium (geranium) cutting is to be taken, a shoot is chosen any time between July and September and is cut off the plant a node lower down than the one needed for making the cutting; for this a cut-and-hold flower gatherer may be used. The shoot is then placed on a level wooden

Making geranium cuttings with one hand using a straight-bladed knife

board with head to the left if the right hand is being used, then with a straight-bladed knife the cut is made just below the node down onto the board. If the Stanley knife with retractable blade is used it can be managed quite well with one hand. Most cuttings root well in a compost of equal parts sand and peat. When rooted they are potted up; the first potting can be into a paper drinking cup which has a hole bored into the base — with loamless compost this is very light to lift and put in position on the bench or in a frame, especially if there is any reaching to be done. As mentioned before, a box with holes in it to take different sized pots keep the latter steady while potting up with one hand or if hands are spastic.

Two groups of cuttings may be taken: the young soft growth of greenhouse plants in which cases heat is often needed, e.g. growing tips of fuchsias; and semi-ripe cuttings which are taken June to August (according to the plant); these include shrubs and invariably root well in a cold frame placed in the shade.

6 Something to Eat

It is very satisfying to eat home grown produce, whether vegetables or fruit, or just interesting herbs for flavouring. There is also the advantage of picking or cutting vegetables just before they are to be cooked; they taste so much better when they are fresh, and also have more food value.

Vegetables

Raised Beds

If vegetables are being grown in a raised bed, the types suitable will be limited, but there is still great enjoyment in eating the produce of the many that can be grown thus.

Siting A 2 foot bed against a wall or fence is not suitable for vegetable growing; a raised bed needs to be out in the open with as much sunlight as possible, otherwise plants become drawn and are far more prone to attacks by pests and diseases with very disappointing results. Siting also needs to be near a supply of water, for the bulk of vegetables consist of water, and soil will dry out more quickly in a raised bed than at ground level. A hose terminating in a handspray which can be regulated is ideal. The bed should be 4 feet wide and approachable from both sides. The length will be determined by the amount the gardener can manage.

Filling Once drainage has been put in the base it is worthwhile buying a few turves to put grass downwards on top of this before filling with soil. These turves will retain the water better than anything else, at the same time allowing any excess to percolate slowly through. 11 in. must be allowed for drainage and turves leaving a depth of 13 in. to be filled with compost or soil for growing vegetables. If the natural underlying soil is gravel the depth of drainage can be less.

The soil for filling may be taken from the garden, if care is taken to remove any perennial weeds. If the garden soil is light and sandy some peat should be added, and whoever is filling the bed needs to mix the soil and peat very thoroughly. If the garden soil tends to be clayey then both peat and sharp sand should be mixed with it. By the second year the soil may have settled and become rather low in the bed; it will then need topping up.

Sowing and planting Because of the comparative shallowness of soil in a raised bed deep-rooting plants such as parsnips are not possible, while Brussels sprouts, sprouting broccoli, and the kales are not only deep rooting but also tall in growth and easily blown over.

Before discussing actual varieties, methods of seed sowing and planting may be mentioned. Rows are best taken lengthwise down the bed, the first row being a few inches from the centre. If the bed is a long one, the row may be only half or even a quarter the length; this planting lengthwise saves going from one side to the other when sowing or planting. Instead of a line, a lath the exact length of the bed, marked in feet and inches can be used; this is put down and held firm by the ends of the bed. If seed sowing, a drill can be made by drawing a sharpened stick along the edge of this lath. A secondary, shorter measuring rod will also be needed, when shifting the first one forward to make the second row. After a while people usually devise a method suitable to themselves. A string line is not advocated as it needs to be absolutely taut, which means moving from end to end when shifting it, and there is rarely sufficient depth of soil to hold the line peg firmly, so that the line easily becomes slack in the process of planting (more so than in seed sowing).

So often far too many plants of one crop are sown or planted at one time e.g. lettuces and cabbages. They all mature about the same time, particularly the lettuces, and many are wasted. It is far more satisfactory to sow and plant

85

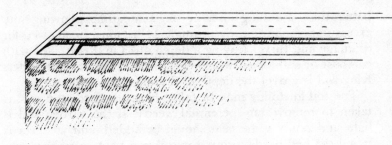

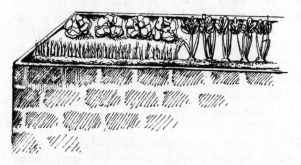

a) *A lath placed in position lengthwise, ready for measuring distances for planting*
b) *Vegetables sown and planted in the raised bed*

little and often.
Suitable Vegetables The following are a few vegetables varieties suitable for a raised bed.
BEETROOT The variety 'Detroit Little Ball' can be used for successional sowing in summer, and 'Sutton's Globe' for storing in winter.
CABBAGE The variety 'Primo' is quite small but has solid heads. The seed is sown in March-April and the plants planted out as soon as they are big enough. Cabbage should be ready to cut July-August. The variety 'Hispi' matures quickly; sown at the same time it can be cut late June.
CARROT 'Parisian Rondo' is a fairly new variety; it is a small rounded carrot which matures quickly and can be sown in succession throughout the season from April onwards. 'Chantenay' is an old favourite of the stump-rooted group, again for use throughout the growing season. 'Scarla' is a

stump-rooted variety grown as a main crop, and will keep throughout the winter.

CELERIAC It would be quite difficult to grow celery in a raised bed, for it needs a deep rich soil and copious water, but celeriac, the turnip-rooted celery, has the same flavour. Freshly dug, it may be grated for salads and is excellent cooked. It does need however to be sown early February March in a cold frame or under a cloche. Sown in boxes it is pricked out and finally planted in May 10 in. apart. It is ready for use in late summer and autumn.

LETTUCE Two varieties admirably suited to growing in a raised tyre bed are 'Tom Thumb' a cabbage type and 'Little Gem' cos type, the latter being the better of the two; both are sown from March to mid-July where they are to continue growing. They are thinned to 4 in. Only sow a few at a time.

ONIONS These can be grown from sets, bought from a garden shop, which are easier to manage. If seed is sown, sow very thinly and thin if necessary to 2 in. apart. Onions require a very fertile soil.

SPINACH gives another 'green' vegetable, but it is not liked by everyone. The varieties 'Greenmarket' and 'Sigmaleaf' are both annuals but if it is sown in the autumn a small picking may be had then followed by further picking in the spring. If it is sown thinly no thinning is needed.

TOMATOES The variety 'The Amateur' is ideal for a raised bed. It needs no side-shooting or staking; it does tend to flop a little, but if it hangs down over the side of the bed the fruits keep beautifully clean. This variety will grow well in a raised tyre bed, but must be in full sun.

TURNIP The variety 'Snowball' is quick growing, round in shape and white in colour; it matures early and is very reliable.

PEAS Maincrop peas grow too tall for a raised bed, also their roots want to delve deep, but early varieties can be grown such as 'Little Marvel' 20 in., and 'Kelvedon Wonder' 18 in. They do sprawl a little so 2 feet needs to be allowed to the next crop.

RUNNER BEANS 'Hammonds Dwarf Scarlet' grows along the ground and needs no staking. It gives excellent beans but it does sprawl so requires plenty of room.

Ground level beds

Many people who are disabled as well as those who are elderly may still wish to grow vegetables at ground level but find difficulty in bending when cultivating the soil. The use of a long-handled hoe, long-handled weed fork or Bestwaye Weeder will keep the ground clean once crops are sown, but it is the initial preparation of the soil which can create a problem. The Wolf handle-grip which can be clamped on to the shaft of a spade or fork helps considerably in lifting the weight of soil with the left hand, prior to turning it over. A professional gardener who after a stroke became hemiplegic was able to dig with one hand with the aid of a handle-grip on his fork. Again, by using the small 'Junior' fork of Stanleys with a handle-grip on it, a person in a wheelchair has managed to dig the soil. For anyone who must remain quite upright there is the Terrex spade (Wolf) which acts on a spring throwing the soil forward with no back-bending. There are however some people who are unable to dig at all. The Wolf soil tiller provides a good tilth by either pushing or

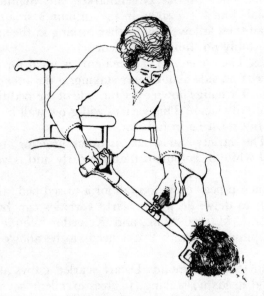

Digging from a wheelchair using a junior fork with handle grip

pulling it through the soil; it is not unduly heavy work and again there is no bending to use it.

For putting down the line preparatory to sowing or planting, two broom handles may be used to which the line is affixed. These handles are sharpened at one end to go into the soil and cut at the other end to a height comfortable for the user. A sharpened broom handle may also be used to take out narrow drills, again obviating bending, or used as a dibber when planting. Holes may be made, then the plants dropped in and firmed with the feet.

A raised bed can of course be comfortable to work at for a person with a bad back who wishes to keep standing. The bed can be built to the required height for the user. Not only the growing but the gathering and harvesting of vegetables is easier when they are grown at a higher level.

Fruit

A fruit orchard is a delightful place, especially in spring. Even one tree can be decorative in that season but if the tree is a standard, half-standard or bush, pruning, general care and finally the picking of the fruit can prove very difficult work and on the whole is not for the elderly or handicapped person.

There are however ways of growing apples and pears which can be managed from an ordinary standing position without stretching, or from a wheelchair — trees grown on the single-stemmed cordon system, or espalier trees; that is, with the branches trained against wires or fences in an horizontal plane. Plums and peaches, because of their different manner of growth, cannot be grown this way.

Choice of tree and rootstock While the apple and pear trees naturally have to be of healthy growth, they must not be too vigorous, otherwise it would be impossible to keep them down to the required size. There are two factors which control the size of the tree, the rootstock and the variety of apple. All fruit tree varieties are grafted on to a rootstock; a vigorous rootstock is chosen for a large orchard tree, a dwarfing rootstock for cordons and espaliers. The choice of variety is again governed by the variety's vigour. 'Bramley's Seedling', the well known cooking apple, for example, is by nature very vigorous; hard pruning to keep the tree small only increases its vigour. The variety 'Lanes' Prince Albert' is much more suitable for a cooking apple. When making a choice good fruit nurseries will always be helpful with advice.

Pollination and Fertilisation A further point for thought before choosing a variety is whether it is self-fertile or requires another variety to pollinate it. If there is to be only one espalier tree a self-fertile variety must be chosen. The Royal Horticultural Society's book *The Fruit Garden Displayed* is very helpful with advice.

Espaliers

The number of tiers of branches spread horizontally will depend on the ultimate height the tree is required to be. Possibly two tiers would be sufficient for people in wheelchairs, while a person standing but not wanting to reach at all there could be three or four. For two or three tiers a really dwarfing rootstock is needed, such as that known as MM106.

Planting Trees are planted 12-15 feet apart. A tree may be purchased already trained but it is far more interesting and absorbing to train the tree oneself. For this a one-year-old tree known as a 'maiden' should be bought. The tree is planted either against a wall or fence where horizontal wires are stretched at one foot intervals between straining eyes. If no fence is available the wires can be stretched against posts put in for the purpose.

Training The training consists of careful pruning, watching the resultant growth. The planting takes place in autumn, so after planting, the maiden is cut back to within 1 foot of the grafting point (which will be found to be quite obvious). In the spring three shoots should grow out; the top one is allowed to go straight up vertically, and the other two are tied out horizontally to the lowest wire, one on either side of the main stem. The vertical shoot will continue growing in the summer, and in the autumn is again cut back to within 1 foot of the horizontal branches; this is continued each year until the required height is obtained, then two shoots only

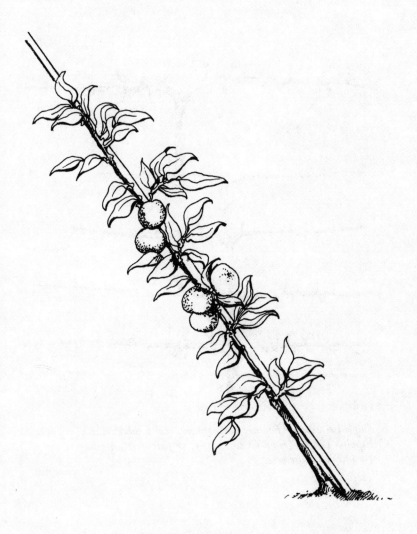

a) *Single cordon apple tree*

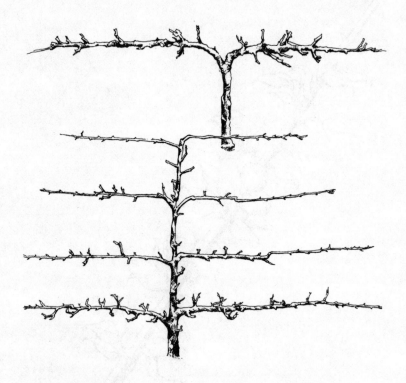

b) *Single tier espalier for easy management from a wheelchair*
c) *Espalier can be grown on two, three, or four tiers according to the gardener's requirements*

are kept and trained out horizontally and the central upright one is cut right out.

General pruning This is done in summer, about the first week in August. The side shoots on the horizontal branches are pruned to about 3 in., cutting back to a bud, after that side shoots are cut to 1 in. to a bud each season. Any unwanted shoots arising on the vertical branch are cut out completely.

Cordons

The rootstocks chosen for cordons are very dwarfing and are named M1X.

Planting This is done in autumn and where the cordons form a row the rows should run from north to south if possible. One-year-old trees are planted 2-3 feet apart at an angle of 45°, with the union where grafted, 4-6 in. above soil level.

Training Each tree is tied to an 8 foot cane; the canes at an angle of 45° are then tied to wires stretched between posts. It is necessary to watch the ties round the trees to ensure that there is no constriction. When the trees reach the top of the canes, the canes are untied from the wires and lowered 10°.

Pruning At planting the main leader is left unpruned, and the side shoots shortened to about 3 in. from the base, cutting to a bud. As with the espalier, annual pruning is done in summer in the latter part of July. New side shoots which arise from the central leader are cut back to about 3 in., always to a bud. The side shoots which were cut back at planting time are now cut to about 1 in. Any secondary growths from these which come after July are cut back in September.

Soft Fruit

Some soft fruits need a great deal of work to grow properly and crop well, such as raspberries, but others can be grown in such a way that their management is easier. Blackcurrants like plenty of mulching, and the cutting out of fruited wood once fruit has been picked. One gardener in a wheelchair had a row of blackcurrants grown alongside a path. When the fruit was ready for picking she cut off the whole stem of fruiting wood with long-armed pruners, then took the whole branches indoors, and picked the fruit off there. Thus the fruit was picked and the bushes pruned in one operation!

Gooseberries can be very difficult with their thick prickly growth, both for pruning and picking. They can however be grown on a stem by taking a hardwood cutting (in autumn) about 8 in. long and removing all the buds except three. The cuttings are inserted about 5 in. of their length into the ground out of doors, with a little sharp sand at their base. When rooted the following year they are transferred to their permanent site. From then on they are allowed to go on growing upwards on a single stem, any side growths being taken out (similar to growing tomatoes). When the desired height is reached the head of the gooseberry is allowed to develop; with a bush like this on a single stem, grown to a convenient height, there need be no bending when picking fruit or pruning. The main stem will need staking as it never thickens greatly and could snap in strong winds. Redcurrants may be treated in the same manner.

Strawberries Normally strawberries grown at ground level, are difficult to pick and they have runners which need to be controlled. A much easier way to grow this fruit is in a barrel, where they can be cared for much more easily.

Drainage is needed down the centre of the barrel as well as at the bottom; for this a piece of piping about 2 in. in diameter is put down the middle and filled with rubble. The rest of the barrel is then filled with soil and the piping withdrawn, leaving a central area of drainage. Holes made in the side of the barrel for strawberry growing should never be less than 2 in. in diameter.

If preparing a barrel is too difficult, or there is no help available, strawberry pots may be bought with the necessary holes cast in the pot. These pots may be placed at whatever level is most convenient to the grower.

Herbs

Parsley, mint, sage and thyme are the standard herbs of most gardens, but of recent years there has been an awakening interest in many others that have been grown in the past.

Originally herbs were collected and grown for their medicinal qualities.

The Romans, and, later, Christian monastries had specialised herb gardens for medicines. Fragrant and culinary herbs were at their peak of cultivation in the time of Elizabeth I. All large houses had their herbary then, not only for medicines but also for flavouring sweetmeats, making sweet scents and for use in cosmetics.

The Royal Botanic Gardens, Kew had its origin in a collection of medicinal plants. The Chelsea Physic Garden was founded in 1673 by the Society of Apothecaries, while in the last war an appeal was made for the collection of herbs in the wild for medicinal purposes, for example, foxglove leaves, burdock, comfrey, dandelion and yarrow.

Culinary herbs have the greatest appeal to the gardener. The word herb has now come to mean a plant that is used in medicine or the kitchen, but originally it just meant 'a plant'. We use the word herbage for the plants along the hedgerows, and more recently the word herbicide for weedkillers.

Growing herbs Herbs can be grown in the mixed border if wished. The purple leaved sage makes a splendid low bush, handsome with other plants. However, if herbs are grown together in one particular bed it is easier for picking and general care. Aromatic herbs thrive best in a light soil and full sun. A raised bed once again is ideal for them because of the perfect drainage which can be obtained, also picking is easy. Many herbs may be grown from seed while others, once a stock plant is bought, can be increased or replaced by taking cuttings.

The following list gives some of the more well known herbs, and they are grouped as perennials, biennials, and annuals.

Perennials Chives are well known with their onion-like leaves growing to 8 in. The rose-mauve flower heads are most decorative but should be removed for the production of more leaves. This is a herb which will flourish in partial shade.

FENNEL, *Foeniculum vulgare*, is a tall plant growing to 6 feet. It has fine feathery leaves which are blue-green in the type, but the bronze leaved form is more beautiful, especially if it is grown with golden sage at its feet. Fennel is not suitable for a raised bed because of its height, also it seeds prolifically and could become a nuisance, so it should only be grown if it can be kept under control by cutting off the flower heads as soon as they appear, to prevent seeding. The leaves are used as a flavouring in sauces.

HYSSOP, *Hyssopus officinalis*, is the hyssop mentioned in the Bible. It is a slightly shrubby perennial growing to about 20 in. and has blue flowers. Both the leaves and the flowers may be used in cooking or in salads; they have a mint-like flavour. Hyssop requires a sunny position and does not become too large for a raised bed. It may be grown from seed.

POT MARJORAM *Origanum onites*, is a relative of the wild plant of the chalk hills. The seed may be sown direct where it is to grow.

MINT There are several mints and the one usually grown is the spearmint *Mentha spicata*. Mint is very vigorous in growth and is certainly not for a raised bed. It is best grown in a bucket sunk in the soil with the rim of the bucket just above soil surface; this prevents the plant spreading and becoming a nuisance.

SAGE, *Salvia officinalis*, is an evergreen shrub with aromatic leaves; the flowers are attractive too, being pale mauve. As the plant originated in the Mediterranean region it needs full sun and a well drained soil. There are varieties which are very decorative, the purple leaved; the gold and green *S.icterina* and *S.officinalis* 'Variegata' with cream, green and purple leaves but this variety is not so strong growing. All three can be used well in a mixed border.

THYMUS VULGARIS, the thyme, makes a small evergreen bush about 12-15 in. high. The leaves are strongly scented; there is a silver variegated variety also a lemon scented one. Thyme can be grown from seed or cuttings; the lemon scented is not as strong growing and is excellent for a raised bed.

Biennial Chervil, *Anthriscus cerefolium*, makes an attractive little plant with fern-like leaves that are aromatic. The seed is sown one year and the plant flowers and seeds the second, but propagates itself by seeding. It is a very easy plant.

Annuals Parsley, *Petroselinum crispum*, is known to everyone as it is so much used for garnishing. There are many legends about it: one that 'The master of the house must sow the seed' and another that the seed has to go down to the devil before it germinates. It is a herb which needs a fertile soil and partial shade. The seed is sown in March.

SUMMER SAVOURY, *Satureia hortensia*, is another herb which will grow well in a raised bed in a sunny position. It only grows to about 9 in., the seed being sown in April.

There are very many other interesting herbs to grow, a reference to books on the subject is made in Appendix 1.

7 Overcoming the Weeds

'One year's seeding, seven years' weeding' — so goes the old saying, and this holds a great measure of truth, especially in the case of some weeds. Weeds in the garden are one of the main problems for all gardeners, but to the disabled person the control of weeds can seem an insuperable task.

There are three main methods of weed control in the garden, cultivating the soil which includes hoeing, the use of ground-cover plants, and the use of herbicides i.e. weed-killers. Some forms of physical disability may permit the use of lightweight and long-reach hoes and cultivators, but for many the use of such tools may be impossible.

Ground Cover

Resort must therefore be made to other kinds of weed control and in many gardens ground-cover plants can be used to great advantage. There has been much interest in the use of certain kinds of ornamental plants as smothering agents and this has become a popular method of weed control in public parks and gardens now that manual labour is so expensive. Ground-cover plants are really weed competitors because they compete with the weeds for light, moisture, and plant foods. Some kinds of ground-cover plants will need nursing during their early years of establishment, at least up until the time that they interlock and form a complete canopy of growth over the soil; herbicides can be used to advantage during this period.

Successful ground-cover subjects could be described as low-growing perennial plants which retain their leaves throughout the whole year (this may include shrubby kinds). There is a very wide range of plants from which to choose; some being choice but expensive and others common and easily propagated and therefore less expensive.

The choice of ground-cover plants will depend upon a number of factors which should be carefully considered. Firstly the soil, whether heavy or light, chalky or acid, stony or sandy, wet or well drained, etc.; then there is the aspect which may be exposed and sunny, shady and sheltered, on a bank or on the level, and finally the nature of the plants themselves. Some plants are slow growing. Others may be strong growing and rampant and can easily become invasive. Obviously one would not plant rampant shrubby kinds on strong fertile soil or, conversely, weak, slow-growing kinds on poor starved soil. A dry stony soil in full sun tends to inhibit the growth of many plants while fertile soil with adequate moisture tends to make plants grow lush and strong, so that they grow beyond the desired area and become as great a problem as the weeds. If possible tour around local parks while examination of local authorities' plantings of traffic roundabouts can be helpful and suggestive of ideas. To make friends with local parks authorities, superintendents, and staff usually evokes a helpful and sympathetic response.

The following list of ground-cover plants made up of perennial plants and shrubs has been carefully chosen with the needs and limitations of disabled gardeners in mind but it must be remembered that soils vary and plants may grow weaker or stronger than expected. Ground-cover plants fall into two main groups, firstly those that spread by sending out runners or suckers, and, secondly, clump-forming kinds that reach a certain size and do not spread further, but only increase in area.

AJUGA REPTANS, Bugle, grows to about 12 in. in height when planted in a moist, partially shaded position. Spreads quickly by runners. *A.r.* 'Atropurpurea' has purple leaves. *A.r.* 'Multicolour' has bronze, cream and pink shaded leaves.

BERGENIA CORDIFOLIA, Elephant Ears, get its common name from the size and shape of the large leaves which are persistent through the winter. Growth is slow and the plant forms clumps with a spread of from 15-24 in. according to variety. In spring there are large trusses of pink flowers. Bergenia will grow in most soils including those with lime; it also grows well in sunny or shady situations and is a most tolerant plant well worth having. The hybrid B. 'Ballawley' has very large leaves and deep pink flowers which are most striking.

BRUNNERA MACROPHYLLA At one time this was listed as anchusa and has the typical forget-me-not-like flowers of deep blue. These are clump-forming plants and are planted 20 in. apart in partial shade. They need moisture in summer.

EUPHORBIA, Spurge, has insignificant flowers but these are surrounded by bracts which are a bright yellowish green which pick up the light of spring sunshine. Two are useful as ground-cover plants. *E.polychroma* (syn.*E.epithymoides*) grows to 18 in. in height. It is evergreen and has brilliant yellow heads of bracts in April-May. This species likes the sun.

E. ROBBIAE has evergreen dark leathery leaves while the bracts are a pale yellow-green. It grows well in shade and plants should be spaced 24 in. apart.

GERANIUM This genus must not be mistaken for the pot-plant and bedding geranium which is really pelargonium. 'Geranium' includes the wild kind which is well known as cranesbill. Among the many garden species there are two which are particularly suitable for ground-cover. *G.endressii* grows 18 in. tall and is clump forming; it prefers a lightly shaded position and bears magenta pink flowers. A very good plant.

G.MACRORRHIZA is an attractive plant with deeply lobed leaves and pale pink flowers set in deep red bracts which persist when the flowers fade. The leaves are slightly aromatic and it is a plant loved by bumble bees. This species will grow and flower in both sunny and shady situations; a good variety is 'Wargrave Pink'. Both these geraniums are well worth having.

HEUCHERA, Coral Bells, has already been mentioned in chapter 5. It is an attractive plant but will not tolerate a heavy clay or badly drained soil.

LAMIUM MACULATUM is a relative of the common dead nettle. It is a spreader but unless on a very rich soil does not become invasive. The dark leaves have a silver stripe down the middle which in the variety 'Roseum' becomes suffused with pink in winter; it also has attractive rose-pink flowers in summer. A very easy plant to grow, to propagate, and to keep under control if necessary. The species *L.galeobdolon*, often advertised for ground cover work, tends to grow too fast and becomes invasive; also it does not have the compact growth and tends to sprawl, giving weeds a chance to grow in between.

STACHYS LANATA, Lambs Ears. The woolly silvery foliage of this plant is well known to most gardeners. It spreads slowly. The variety 'Silver Carpet' has no flowers and makes a compact covering over the soil, remaining so all the winter. It is not suitable for growing in the north or in cold wet districts.

ERICA, Heather. Most heathers like an acid soil but the winter flowering group *E.carnea* and *E.darleyensis* grow and flower well on soils containing lime. They make excellent thick coverage and while better for clipping over when flowers have finished in order to make them more bushy, will thrive without such attention. Ericas are best planted 12 in. apart in autumn or spring, some peat being added when planting. The following varieties of *Erica carnea* are given in flowering succession: 'Praecox Rubra', December-March, deep red; 'King George', January-April, rich rosy-pink; 'Aurea', February-April, golden foliage, pink flowers; 'Vivelli', February-May, very bright carmine flowers; 'Springwood Pink', January-March, pink flowers.

EUONYMUS FORTUNEI 'Radicans Varigatus'. This small leaved trailing shrub makes good ground cover. It is evergreen and the leaves which are greyish-green have a white margin which often turns pink.

HEBE These are the shrubby veronicas. One which is very suitable for ground cover and which forms a mat-like covering of silver leaved branches is *H.pinguifolia* 'Pagei' and is sometimes listed in catalogues as *H. pageana*. It spreads slowly and has leaves which are very small but closely packed. This is a good plant to have near the edge of a path as it is slow growing and unlikely to spread too far over the paving. It is attractive throughout the year and bears small white flowers in May.

HEDERA HELIX, the common ivy, makes good ground cover, but it will need to be cut back at times. *H.h.* 'Buttereup' is a golden form of *H.h.* 'Caenwoodiana' which has small green leaves deeply divided.

HYPERICUM CALYCINUM, Rose of Sharon, is a long-lived, dwarf evergreen shrub which can spread rather rapidly. It makes excellent ground cover and is suitable for sites where the soil is both dry and shaded and it is difficult to get anything else to grow. It is often seen on banks as it holds the soil together. This plant has large golden saucer shaped flowers with many stamens. It flowers in summer and is visited by many insects.

MAHONIA AQUIFOLIUM This shrub is known as the Oregon Grape by reason of its attractive dark blue berries. It will grow to about 3 feet tall and has evergreen shiny leaves comprised of several leaflets which turn reddish bronze in winter. There are clusters of scented yellow flowers borne in March and April. This plant spreads by suckers, but it is not rampant and will grow in most soils both in sunny and shady situations. The leaves are useful in winter for flower arrangements; this is a good handy all-rounder.

SENECIO LAXIFOLIA is a low spreading shrub of about 2½ feet in height with soft grey leaves and bright yellow daisy-like flowers in summer. The grey foliage shows to advantage when planted in full light.

THYMUS DRUCEI *(T.serphyllum)* is very small leaved plant which is aromatic and will quickly spread over the surface of the soil (provided it is not clay) forming a thin mat. Patches sometimes tend to die away but young pieces can be broken off and inserted to fill the gaps. This plant is not recommended for large areas, but for small spaces which need to be filled near the house or alongside a path, where after bruising it will scent the air.

VINCA MAJOR, periwinkle. is an old favourite with its blue flowers. It is vigorous and is inclined to be rampant in small restricted areas. Perhaps for such situations a better form to plant is the lesser periwinkle *V.minor* Variegata which has cream variegated leaves and the typical blue flowers. This form is easily controlled and will thrive in sun and partial shade.

Herbicides

While effective control of weeds can be obtained in certain situations by the use of ground-cover plants there will remain other areas where weeds need to be controlled by other means. It is in such situations that herbicides may well be used to advantage. There is a vast number of herbicides in common use in agriculture and gardens; most of them are selective and specific in action. Few of these are suitable for use by disabled gardeners even if obtainable. Most herbicides are used by diluting a concentrated liquid in water and applying this to the area to be treated by means of a sprayer, watering-can or some other special appliance. This procedure demands the use of relatively large quantities of water, which can cause difficulties.

Fortunately there are three herbicides available in granular form and these are offered for sale in sprinkler canisters of a size suitable for holding in one hand and it only remains for the user to sprinkle the granules over the soil surface. Each of these holds possibilities for disabled gardeners. They are different in effect and each one should be used only for the purposes described.

DICHLOBENIL This chemical is obtainable at garden centres and similar places by the proprietary name 'Casoron G'. This weedkiller is intended for use in total weed control on land not intended for cropping e.g. around buildings, on drives, roads, and paths. It can also be used for the control of couch grass, perennial nettles, and a number of species of perennial weeds round apples, pears, blackcurrants, gooseberries, roses and most ornamental plants. It should only be used around *established* fruit, roses and ornamentals.

PROPACHLOR This herbicide is readily available at garden centres and main stores under the proprietary name 'Ramrod'. It is intended for the control of annual weeds arising from seed and is no use for controlling established perennial weeds. It can be used to control seedling weeds between onion, leeks and brassica crops and also weeds between ornamental plants including bedding plants. The best way to use this weedkiller is to sprinkle the granules over the soil surface immediately following bedding-out. This herbicide must never be used on recently sown seeds or in the kitchen garden or on the annual flower border. It will control all weeds arising from seeds for a period of six weeks.

SIMAZINE This herbicide is also available in a granular formulation suitable for sprinkling on to soil or path surfaces. It should be applied to the area before weeds appear and will control all weeds arising from seed. It is much more persistent than propachlor and must be used only on paths or around established shrubs and trees, the only exception to this being sweet corn. It is a very useful herbicide for use around raspberries and blackcurrants, also gooseberries, but must not be used around newly planted strawberries. There are a number of liquid herbicides which can be diluted in water and applied through a 'sprinkler bar' or 'dribble bar' which is an attachment for use with a watering can and enables the herbicide to be used between growing plants and eliminates the risk of damage from spray drift. It cannot be over-emphasised that reading directions for use before attempting to open the product is essential. Probably the most widely used liquid herbicide is paraquat; this with the closely related diquat is used for destroying the ariel parts of weeds without affecting the soil. This type of weedkiller, used through a 'sprinkler bar' is easier than hoeing between rows of vegetables or between flowers. A mixture of simazine, diquat and paraquat is a very popular herbicide for use on paths, and is sold under the trade name 'Pathclear'.

Lawns

Most people like a lawn to look at; grass 'is easy on the eye' and makes an excellent setting for many plants, but if the care of a lawn is difficult to maintain, it is best kept to a minimum in size, or may be dispensed with altogether.

Lawns are more than 'patches of grass'. Lawns consist of hundreds of plants, each one being grass of a particular species which needs as much care and attention as any in the flower border to obtain good results.

The lawn exacts more hard work from a gardener than any other part of the garden. Unlike the rest of the garden it cannot be redesigned to suit a specific disability. Mowing has to be done of necessity and this can be done much more easily than in the past by reason of the design of modern lawn mowers using electric power; but there is also the task of sweeping and aerating the lawn, and the application of top-dressing in autumn to be done. The control of weeds and moss also presents an extra task. The easy way to do top dressing and control weeds in one operation is to obtain some combined top dressing and weedkiller and to sprinkle this over the lawn as directed. Moss control is effected by feeding the lawn regularly and not mowing the lawn too closely. Existing patches of moss can be eradicated by the use of a proprietary moss killer. Some brands are based on organo mercury which is poisonous, but non-poisonous kinds are available, particularly one based on dichlorophen.

Many of the modern lawn mowers are light in weight and some small electric powered mowers have only one handle. Electric mowers are of two main types viz. battery operated and mains operated. Mains operated types necessitate the use of a trailing cable which requires a certain knack or technique in handling to avoid cutting it with the mower; battery operated types do not have this disadvantage but are heavier and the battery must be recharged each time the mower is used.

Mowers with rotary blades are also popular, and the Flymo has been used by a person in a wheelchair whose upper limbs are strong, swinging the machine in a semicircular movement.

When cutting the grass it will be found easier if the corners of the lawn are rounded instead of being at right angles, the machine being thus much easier to guide.

Long-armed shears can be used for edging, or a powered lawn edger that may be used with one hand; this has either a cable to the mains or a battery to be charged. The grass cuttings can be lightly swept along the gulley then picked up with the 'Anita Grab' so saving back bending.

The more difficult part of lawn maintenance is aerating it. There are machines for this, but they are heavy to push, while power driven ones prove expensive when they are only used once a year.

Perhaps the easiest way of having an area of grass is to 'rough-cut' it with a rotary cutter, rather than maintain a perfect lawn.

8 Gardening Indoors

Balcony

Flat dwellers often have a balcony, even if only a small one, where it is pleasant to be on a sunny day; pleasanter still if it is colourful with plants and flowers.

One enlightened London Borough has council flats for the elderly and handicapped people and they are set in a well designed area of grass, shrubs, trees and flowers and each flat has a balcony or window box. The tenants are supplied with free John Innes compost the first year of tenancy and thereafter every fifth year. The result is that everyone grows plants of some sort so that non-residents often walk through to enjoy the flowers and the beauty of the area. There are some self-appointed wardens (residents) who tidy up any litter and keep an eye open for vandalism.

Before deciding on containers and what to grow, advice should be sought on the amount of weight the balcony can take. Having ascertained this, plans may be made. Most containers are very light (even when they appear heavy as the simulated lead ones do) as they are made of fibreglass and similar materials.

A good garden container can be adapted from the encasing of moulded polystyrene used for certain articles. These moulded cases are extremely light in weight to place in position, and because of the articles they were moulded round, they are often of unusual shape holes for drainage are easily made with a metal skewer.

Plant containers need to be set at any height suitable to the gardener, but if levels can vary a little the balcony will look more interesting. If a jardiniere (a trough on legs) is used indoors for house plants it will be found that if castors are put on the feet, it can be pushed on to the balcony quite easily and the plants enjoy the air.

While the flat-dweller will want as many plants as possible, enough space must be left for free movement. If suitable wall space is available this may be used for climbing plants. Netlon can be affixed to the wall for the plants to grow up, with containers at the foot to take the plants. The containers need to be 18 in. deep so that there is room for drainage at the base and enough compost not to dry out too quickly. If the containers used are stood over plastic trays, it does save a wet (and possibly slippery) balcony when watering. If annual plants such as Canary creeper, or nasturtiums are used, the container may be quite small in width. Canary creeper has prettily shaped fresh green leaves with small yellow flowers and will flourish even on a north facing wall; once it has started growth it needs no training except the tucking in of an occasional stray shoot. Nasturtiums need the sun; south or west walls are best for them. Both these plants may be grown from seed sown directly into the container in spring. Canary creeper is quite trouble free, but nasturtiums can sometimes be rather shy of flowering. As these plants die before the winter there is no fear of them growing beyond reach and becoming out of hand, as ivy might do.

Further flowers may be grown in hanging baskets, the baskets can be on a pulley so that they are above head height, but can be let down for watering and general care. Already it can be seen that there can be flowers around without using much floor space.

If buying compost there are many pre-packed loamless ones which are light and easy to handle, but filling even a small container can be quite expensive. The compost will last several years however provided the plants are given fertiliser each year.

Planting may be much the same as given for the patio garden minus any trees or shrubs. A miniature rose garden may be had with the dwarf varieties, and the balcony area makes a good setting for it. Ivies trailing over the edge of containers will give some green for the winter months, but are best used only as trailers, for once they begin to climb they will entail much work which may be impossible to cope with.

Window Boxes

Window boxes make delightful small gardens in miniature and they can be cared for from indoors provided there are sash windows. For casement windows brackets may be put on the wall so that the top of the plants grown are level with the opening window; but this is not at all suitable for working from indoors as it is far too difficult to stretch down and reach the plants both for planting and caring for them.

There are several types of window boxes available, those of fibreglass being very light and very durable. The box should not be more than 1 in. wider than the windowsill, otherwise the weight of soil could make the box topple forward. If the window is one or more storey up a plastic tray underneath the box is advisable to prevent drips on any windows underneath. As sills slope forwards slightly, a wedge underneath the front edge of the box will be necessary, not only to bring it level but to make it firm. A wire going round the front of the box and affixed to the window frame each side is a further safeguard.

The compost to be used will depend on what the gardener can manage. Soil from the garden (or a friend's garden) can be used, in a mixture with an equal part of peat. Alternatively a loamless compost (pre-packed) is light and easy to carry, but if this is used the plants will need feeding throughout the summer after the first four weeks of growth.

Plants There are many plants which can be grown in a window box. In spring easy to grow and delightful to see are the many miniature bulbs. Scillas and chionodoxas, crocus and in particular the species and miniature daffodils mentioned in chapter 2. All these will give a spring display year after year, a refreshing sight after the winter months. Easy-care plants for the summer months are the fibrous rooted begonia (this may be taken indoors as a house plant in the winter) the half-hardy annuals mentioned in chapter 5, tagetes, petunias and busy lizzie. All these once planted will be found very good tempered, they are popular plants and usually easily obtainable. When planting any type of flowers it is worth buying a packet of night-scented stock seed, there is nothing attractive about the plant as it looks more like a weed, but the scent in the evening with the window open makes it a 'must'. Between other plants it is not noticeable but the scent can be enjoyed. If there is room indoors during the winter months to keep a few pelar-goniums (geraniums) the miniature ones look very well in a window box and due to their small size quite a variety may be planted.

If permanent planting is wanted the miniature roses are worth considering; they do not need the ordinary rose pruning, so there are no wide open windows on a cold day. Their pruning consists of cutting the flowering stems well back when the flowers are over. Herbs are another group of plants that can be grown, provided the right ones are chosen i.e. those which do not grow too tall or spread too rapidly. Thymes are suitable and if the silver or golden forms are chosen they look more attractive. Chives is another herb that keeps within bounds, also summer savory and the sub-shrubby hyssop with blue flowers; all are suitable for the area available. If there is an interest in growing vegetables, the 'rondo' type of carrot will succeed well, as also 'Little Gem' and 'Tom Thumb' lettuces and the inevitable radishes.

Indoor Plants

Plants for growing indoors are legion, but the choice is governed by various factors, first the amount of light in the room and which aspect it faces, then the type of heating, whether the whole house is heated or not; then of course there is the question of what the handicapped person can manage. It is not always easily grown plants that are chosen. For instance the rubber plant *Ficus robusta* grows well almost unattended in a centrally heated room except for watering, but it grows tall and big and eventually it can reach the ceiling. The plant cannot be controlled by cutting back as this would spoil it, also once it is put in place it is far too heavy to shift, let alone repot.

When buying a new plant it is as well to ask the size it will grow to. Plants need to be small enough to be within the ability of the grower to manage.

The majority of house plants do well if a group of plants are plunged in peat, still in their pots, in a large bowl or trough. The peat is kept moist so giving the right atmosphere around the plants. With this method, any individual plant can be taken out and replaced by another if wished.

A big difficulty for some handicapped people is watering; unlike in a greenhouse, there cannot be capillary watering for any attractive bowl that happens to be in the house. If water has to be carried, some people prefer to use a milk bottle for both carrying the water and watering the plant. The grip is at the top with the weight of water below and can be more controllable than a watering can where the weight of water comes in front of the hand and wrist.

Some people have jardinieres which are like troughs on

A plant trough on castors for mobility

legs. It is useful to be able to sit and tend the plants in these and they have added value in that if castors are put on the feet the jardiniere can be pushed to the sink (even used perhaps, as a walking aid) which is far easier than carrying water to the plants, and if any water is spilt in the kitchen it does not matter so much. An added usefulness is that the jardiniere is easily placed where the light is most suitable for the time of year.

There are several groups of plants which may be grown indoors. There are foliage plants, flowering plants, succulents and cacti and bulbs.

The foliage plants, on the whole, come from warmer countries than ours, tropical or semi-tropical forests where there is a canopy of trees above them so they are rarely in direct sunlight. A centrally heated room has much the same temperature as those forests, the only difference is that our rooms have a much drier atmosphere, and the humidity is what the plants miss.

CHLOROPHYTUM ELATUM, the spider plant, is quite well known. The long grass-shaped leaves are a cream colour edged with green. It is a plant that will stand neglect, but naturally looks better for a little care. It will grow in light or in shade. As the plant becomes older it sends out long stems with little plantlets at the end; when allowed to grow uninterrupted, trailing down from the parent plant, these are most effective. These same plantlets may be cut or broken off and potted up, when they will form a new plant. Some of them consist of a single shoot others a triple or double; the latter two make the better new plant. It can be propagated in this way when it becomes too big.

FATSHEDERA LIZEI, has no common name; it is a cross between an ivy and the Fatsia or castor oil plant. Fatshedera is very easy to grow, especially where there is no central heating, in fact it does not require a very warm temperature. Unlike the rubber plant it may be cut back without spoiling the plant; it also grows well in the darker parts of a room.

HEDERA HELIX ivy. The wild ivy growing on the woodland floor is an engaging little plant, especially when the leaves have a reddish tinge. There are very many varieties of this plant all of which are easy to grow and propagate. *H.h.* 'Saggitifolia' has small deeply divided leaves like fingers; *H.h.* 'Cristata' is sometimes known as the holly ivy with its crested leaves; these and other plain green varieties will grow in the darker parts of a room. The variegated varieties such as *H.h.* 'Glacier' and *H.h.* 'Chicago' also grow easily but need more light otherwise they lose their variegations.

Should ivies become too rambling indoors after a time, they can be cut back or are easily propagated by layering at any time of the year. Just lay a growing stem on a pot filled with soil and peg the stem down with a hair pin or even put a light weight on the stem to keep it in contact with the soil. Once rooted it may be cut from the main plant which can then be thrown away if wished.

Ivies are fascinating plants with many variations, and are so easy to care for that quite a collection can be made of them whether the house is centrally heated or not, as they are normally quite hardy.

PEPEROMIA CAPERATA is a beautiful little plant, with small heart-shaped crinkly leaves. It grows best when there is central-heating and is more difficult to grow where there are greater fluctuations in temperature. Care needs to be taken when watering that the leaves do not become too wet; a steady hand is needed. This plant requires good light but should not be placed in full sunlight.

PHILODENDRON SCANDENS comes from Mexico and is a climber, with small heart-shaped leaves, smooth and of a pleasant green. It looks well climbing up a frame; it requires good light but not direct sun, and can be propagated the same way as the ivy.

SANSEVIERIA LAURENTII, known as Mother-in-laws-Tongue, is at its best when it is neglected. It is a native of tropical Africa. As a room plant watering is best forgotten except when new growth is seen, and even then it only needs a small quantity. It will soon collapse beyond recovery with even the normal 'moderate' watering; this cannot be over-emphasised. It is a most useful plant for the person who has periods when he is unable to tend to his plants. The long 'tongue' or leaf has an almost chevron pattern of dark and light green and grows to 2 feet at least.

SAXIFRAGA SARMENTOSA is the Mother-of-Thousands; like

the spider plant it throws out small plantlets but they are far more numerous in this case. The plant comes from China and Japan. It grows forming a rosette of leaves which are rounded and dark green but pink underneath; the runners are pink in colour and the plantlets are the same as the parent, so the whole is quite colourful, though it does flower. This is another easy plant, but is not for the window sill where the sun will scorch the leaves. It is propagated by the little plantlets.

THE TRADESCANTIAS are named after John Tradescant, a plant collector who is buried at St Mary's churchyard next to Lambeth Palace. These plants are probably the easiest to grow, and it is not always realised how many different varieties there are, thus a person who has very little ability with the arms and hands could make a colourful collection of tradescantias. They are very simple to propagate; where with most plants, when taking a cutting one is told to 'make a clean cut below a joint' with tradescantias this is not at all necessary. A young growth can be broken off just however it can be managed at no specific point. If this cutting is put in a loamless compost and kept watered it will soon root. These plants will grow in the darker part of a room, but do then tend to become a little leggy, and do not have quite such a good colour. The following are tradescantias with their 'cousins' which will make a very colourful group for the person who wishes to grow plants but has minimum dexterity.

T.FLUMINENSE 'Variegata' has small leaves of pale green with a paler stripe which sometimes has a mauvish colour in it.

T.F.AUREA has yellow striped leaves of quite a strong colour.

T.ALBIFLORA 'Tricolor' is of a trailing habit and has leaves of green, white and pink. It bears white flowers. T. 'Quicksilver' is of strong growth with leaves silver and green striped, and these colours remain even if the plant has to be grown away from the light. This plant is of upright habit.

T.BLOSSFELDIANA is of erect habit with woolly green leaves (quite different from the other tradescantias) which are pink underneath.

SETCREASIA PURPUREA is very erect, almost stiff, but does not grow tall. The lance shaped leaves are greenish purple above and bright purple below, glowing when the sun shines through them. It does flower, the blooms being a delicate mauve, making the plant look very handsome. This setcreasia will stand very many weeks without water; it is true that after this it does go rather brown and look weary, but when watered again new shoots will come from which cuttings may be taken.

ZEBRINA PURPUSSII has leaves which are green above and purple beneath, but a different purple from the setcreasia.

ZEBRINA PENDULA is a trailing plant as the name implies and a very good one too. It has purplish leaves with bands of silver and green on the upper surface and is most handsome; the colour is spoilt, turning rather brown, if the plant is left in full sunlight. It is best near the window but not right in it. When the trails become too long with the loss of leaves nearer the base of the stem, the tip can be broken off to start a new plant.

These plants or some of them grouped together in a bowl or trough give a most pleasing effect with their differing coloured leaves and habits of growth. Anyone who has never attempted to grow house plants before should try the tradescantias; they are most rewarding.

Flowering Plants

PELARGONIUM is perhaps the easiest of all flowering plants to grow. It is usually wrongly called geranium and is often seen in cottage windows. It likes as much sun as possible and does not need much water in winter. The same plant can be kept year after year, if cut back in March each year, at which time watering is increased and a little fertiliser given, that is, if re-potting is not possible. Cuttings may be taken July-September or in March as they root best in these months. Cuttings are not difficult to make, as the stems are large and can be laid on a flat piece of wood where the joint is easily seen and a cut made just below it, with one hand if necessary. Cuttings can be put three to a 2½ in. pot in a mixture of equal parts peat and sand, and watered sparingly until rooted. Miniature pelargoniums can form a good collection for the indoor windowsill. They do not need great heat; just as long as the room is frost-proof in winter they will survive.

IMPATIENS SULTANII, Busy Lizzie, is a very popular plant. It flourishes in its young stage, but tends to die out as it becomes older. Propagation is simple in water. This is done by placing a piece of card completely over the top of a small jar (a potted meat one would do) which contains water. A small hole is made in the card through which the stem of a young shoot of Busy Lizzie is inserted. It is fascinating to watch the roots appear and continue growing, and as soon as there are sufficient the plant is potted up.

SAINTPAULIA IONANTHA, the African violet, is a very popular plant, and while it is a little more faddy in its needs, it can be propagated the same way as the Busy Lizzie, in water, except only a single leaf with the leaf stalk is used. A small plantlet will form at the base of the leaf stalk, and when large enough it is cut off and potted on, and the leaf stalk returned to the jar to form another plantlet. African violets require a humid atmosphere, so they grow well on a shelf above the kitchen sink, provided it is not by a window facing full south. They prefer the light of a north or east window, but not a south or west one.

BEGONIA. The small fibrous rooted begonia that has been used as a bedding plant, whether in a window box or raised bed, may be lifted in the autumn and potted up and kept indoors as a house plant. At first shoots will die back due to the sudden change, but gradually new growth will appear. Watering should be moderate until growth is well started; the amount needed will depend on the temperature of the room. These are very rewarding plants, as having given colour all the summer, after a rest they will continue to do so indoors during the winter. Any dead growth should be cut out with knife or scissors, otherwise a rot may set in.

Succulent plants

Succulents are easy plants provided they can be kept right in a south window; their main need is a good light. While cacti, which of course are a type of succulent, are very interesting, they are very prickly for handling, taking off-sets etc. Many succulents are easy to hold because their curious shape give something to grip. One favourite is the partridge alow, *A.variegata* with striped green and cream leaves. The 'Mexican hat', *Bryophyllum daigremontianum*, has broad leaves like the brim of a hat, and each leaf on maturity has tiny plantlets all round the edge. The plant can grow to 3 feet, flowers and then dies, but the tiny plantlets drop off the leaf edges and take root where they fall.

LITHOPS are the 'mimicry pebble' plants. In South Africa, their home, during the dry weather, they shrink down into the soil, their flat tops looking just like pebbles. When the rains come the plants start to grow, the 'pebble' splits in two and a flower emerges. These plants grow well from seed, but they need plenty of light for flowering; however they are fascinating even without flowers.

SEDUM RUBROTINCTUM, is an indoor sedum whose leaves are red, and can be propagated by a piece of stem or just one small leaf.

Many succulents can give pleasure, as provided they have enough light, they are undemanding, while should they have to be left for quite a long period, they will not die, even if they look a little sorry for themselves.

Bulbs

Most people like to have some bulbs flowering in the home, in spring especially the hyacinth with the delicate scent. Hyacinths may be grown in water using specially made glasses, so that the roots may be watched growing. Growing in fibre is not recommended as an outdoor temperature is required for root growth.

Crocus can be grown indoors but are best in a room where there is no heat, then they are brought into the warmth when the flower buds appear. Purple crocus are easier to grow indoors than yellow ones. For people who have a spare room which is unheated, or have a sun room, some of the South African bulbs are very beautiful in their flowers and do not need much attention other than watering.

Daffodils and hyacinths in fibre are not recommended as they need an outdoor temperature for root growth and are then brought indoors for flowering, which is often more than a handicapped person can manage.

LACHENALIAS, known as 'Cape cowslips' are more like our bluebell in shape but are basically yellow in colour. They grow to about 8 in. — *L.aureum* has clear golden bells, *L.tricolor* has yellow bells with a red and a green stripe at the edge. These bulbs may be planted in August-September five bulbs to a 3 in. pot. They are watered when planted and then left until the first shoot appears; watering is increased as growth is made. They grow best at a temperature of 45°F and can be brought into the living room when flowers begin to show. When the flowers finish, the leaves are allowed to die gradually by reducing watering, while the bulbs may be left in the pot until they are started up again in fresh compost the following September. Potting up and watering are the only things needed for these beautiful flowers, provided they can be grown in the cool.

BABIANA, the baboon root, is so called because baboons found the corms of these plants good to eat. They are not very well known in this country, but they are available and the treatment is much the same as for lachenalias. The leaves have a pleated appearance and the cup shaped flowers often open to a star shape; they are in colours of blue, mauve and white. These bulbs are very well worth trying. They are something new to have, and demand very little work, but they cannot be grown in a centrally heated house with full success.

Watering of house plants This can be one of the most difficult things in growing house plants as no set rule may be given. On the whole water less in winter and only increase watering when it can be seen that new growth is starting. Always water sparingly rather than overwater. So many house plants need a humid atmosphere rather than watering, and this is why plunging in damp peat can help overcome the problem. The peat must only be kept damp and not soaking wet.

Growing plants in water One way of overcoming the watering problem is to grow plants in water. This of course is only possible with certain plants. As mentioned previously there are several plants where cuttings will root in water, and they will continue to grow if given a liquid fertiliser, but instead of a jar an attractive bowl or dish can be used. Even a circular decorated margarine tub will serve and it is light to handle.

Plants growing in pebbles and water, using any interesting container from around the house

In the container are placed a few pieces of charcoal, obtainable from a florist or shop which caters for barbecues. Over the charcoal the dish is filled with washed pebbles from the garden, or a friend's garden. Cuttings of Busy Lizzie, the tradescantias, plantlets of spiderwort and 'Mother of Thousands' can be tucked in between the pebbles then the dish filled two-thirds of its depth with water. The dish will need topping up with water once a week. Once the cuttings and plantlets have rooted, a drop of liquid feed may be given once a fortnight. The amount rather depends on the size of the dish and number of plants in it. Too much fertilizer will make the plants grow too large too quickly. A dish of plants can last two years at least. As the plants grow taller the tops can be nipped off for further cuttings, thus making the original plants more bushy. This is a very easy way to grow certain house plants which presents no watering problem.

9 The Greenhouse and Garden Shed

A heated greenhouse can be a fascinating place, a small world of its own with a different climate from the garden outside, warmer in winter but sometimes very hot in summer.

Heating throughout the winter months at only 45°F can produce a wide variety of pot plants for the garden, vegetables as well as flowers and a good display in the greenhouse itself. A greenhouse is somewhere interesting to retreat to; even on a dreary winter day there is always something that needs to be done.

The choice of greenhouse for anyone who has a handicap is of paramount importance. It is advisable to consult catalogues of several different firms before making a final choice to suit the individual need. The choice of material, wood or metal, is purely personal, though metal (aluminium) is virtually indestructible. It is the door and doorway which are important. A finger-tip sliding door is by far the easiest to manage, added to which there is no possibility of the door banging and glass breaking.

The doorway needs to be wide enough for the use of a walking frame or wheelchair, with no barrier of any kind at ground level, but a smooth run-in for a wheelchair, and nothing to catch the toe on when walking. A larger sized greenhouse may have to be bought, not only because of the entrance, but also because of the need for a broad path inside; this path should be level, smooth and firm, preferably concrete or paving slabs, neither of which are usually advocated in a greenhouse because it is better to 'damp down' in summer on an absorbent surface, but in this case safety comes first combined with ease of movement.

Once inside the greenhouse small alterations and possibly additions can be made. For anyone in a wheelchair or sitting to work the normal bench height is often a little high, and the arms of the gardener have to be raised too much so that working is both uncomfortable and tiring; the bench therefore is best lowered a little, enough to allow the arms of a wheelchair to go underneath. For those who are not very strong and find leaning forward difficult a narrower bench of 18 in. is often more suitable, otherwise plants at the back of the bench are just out of reach, which is always most exasperating. Most firms have narrow benching which is sold normally for the smallest greenhouses.

The most suitable source of heat is electricity; once installed, the operation is both reliable and simple to manage. A thermostat must be part of the installation in order to maintain a pre-set temperature with a minimum of waste heat. Care must be taken in the erection of the greenhouse to ensure that all sections fit closely together, and that ventilators close properly in order to avoid draughts and loss of heat.

The thermostat should be placed within easy reach and set at the minimum temperature to maintain healthy growth for the kind of plant being grown. For many plants 45°F is sufficient. Some cheaper sources of heating are available with the added advantage of freedom from electricity power cuts. 'Bottled' gas has recently come into favour and provided a supplier is available who will replace the new cylinder as required, it may well prove cheaper than electricity.

Until recently, more difficult than heating the greenhouse has been ventilating it. There are now automatic ventilating units; the majority do not open ventilators at regulated temperatures, but work on the following principle. There is a hinged arm to the ventilator, at the base of which there is a section which holds a chemical, this chemical when the weather becomes hot expands and so pushes up the arm of the ventilator, thus opening it. Towards evening as the temperature cools so does the chemical and the ventilator automatically closes. This automatic ventilation is a boon, even if the owner is only out for a few hours and the weather turns warm after a grey start; the ventilators will open so avoiding scorch to many plants.

Further automation is for watering. This is of vital importance especially if the greenhouse has to be left occasionally or when the owner is on holiday. It does take away some of the interest as the correct watering for different plants is part of the skill in learning to grow them. However automation is very helpful particularly where arms and hands are not strong or there is spasticity in the upper limbs. Watering can be very difficult to control with a watering can because of the water's movement within the can, consequently one plant can have too much water, another none at all or not enough; there are days when just the minimum of water is needed, so control over the watering can is necessary.

There are several different kinds of automatic watering units on the market, and the capillary matting type is one of the easiest to use. There are firms which sell the complete outfit of water tank, water trough and matting, the latter absorbing the water which is then taken up through the base of plastic plant pots.

There is a D.I.Y. method which is comparatively cheap. Polythene sheeting is laid along the bench; at the centre of the bench a hole is cut just large enough to let in an ordinary baking tin. On the polythene are laid strips of the capillary matting, the ends of which dip into the baking tin. This baking tin has to be kept topped up with water which is absorbed by the matting, then through the pots standing on it to the plants. Plastic pots must be used, if only clay ones are available then a 'wick' of capillary matting is put into the hole at the bottom. When topping up the tin it does not matter if water splashes on the matting, it is just absorbed. If shading is needed a spray in aerosol form is easy to put on the glass but very difficult to remove, particularly for anyone with a handicap. Blinds though expensive are much better, and could possibly be used one side only according to the position of the greenhouse. An important point is to make sure that the cords of the blinds are long enough for easy

121

D.I.Y. method of watering plants with capillary matting

reach and handling.

However attractive a greenhouse may look there comes a time when it needs to be cleaned down thoroughly. Insect pupae will overwinter in any crevice, even in a metal house, while spores from fungal diseases can overwinter on wood-work and in the soil, so some attempt at cleaning is most necessary. One thing that minimises cleaning is by having as little as possible stored under benches, such as odd boxes, pieces of sacking etc., as these provide an overwintering home for unwanted guests. If the greenhouse is kept as simple and uncluttered as possible it will help in some measure towards cleanliness. The best time to clean a greenhouse is when the stock of plants is at the lowest. It is not advisable for handicapped people to use many of the modern chemicals for cleaning, such as the emulsified cresylic acid, unless they have *perfect* control in pouring out and using the liquid. Protective clothing of course should be worn anyway. A safe liquid to use is Jeyes' Fluid.

The first step in cleaning is to brush down with a dry broom and get rid of as much debris as possible, and follow this by a wash down of the house and benches with Jeyes'

Fluid; this again may be done with a broom from a sitting position if the arms are strong enough. Jeyes' Fluid is quite harmless to the user and to any plants; some plants may have just been pushed to one side but splashing should not hurt them. If there is a ground level bed this may be soaked with the Jeyes' which has a beneficial rather than a harmful effect on the soil. Directions are on the container and Jeyes publish a leaflet on the use of their product in gardening.

If it is not possible for the gardener to do this cleaning himself he should try and obtain some help so the cleaning can at least be done every other year.

Plants for a greenhouse with a winter temperature of 45°F are almost endless. Pelargoniums (geraniums), both the old plants and cuttings taken in August, may be overwintered, while many pot bulbs prefer this temperature to a centrally heated house. Vegetable seeds started early in the year such as cabbage, leeks and celeriac find it acceptable, also the half-hardy annuals mentioned in chapter 5.

During the summer tomatoes may be grown. If they are planted at ground level, some handicapped people will be unable to care for them, as there will be too much bending taking out side shoots etc. If grown in 'Tom-bags' the latter can be placed at any height convenient for the grower, and to prevent the plants growing too tall and out of reach, two growths or even three may be taken up instead of the usual one. These shoots may be fanned out sideways then stopped at a height convenient for the grower; in this way they can be cared for sitting down. Tom-bags do require quite a deal of water and after about a month the tomatoes will need feeding.

There are many good books on general greenhouse management, but the important point is to have the necessary adaptations so that control over heating, watering and ventilation is maintained without unnecessary exertion.

Frames

Cold frames are extremely useful, particularly when no greenhouse is available. Half-ripe cuttings of many shrubs will root easily in a cold frame in June-July. It can be used for rock plant cuttings, also for sowing seed a week or two earlier than out in the garden. Frames can be very awkward to manage, as they are usually sited at ground level and the light has to be pushed back to open the frame, which means leaning forward to pull it back for closing, usually a difficult posture. A frame with a hinged light is easier to open, and if the frame is fixed firmly on to a table at the required height, then the frame may be used with the minimum of back bending, or from a wheelchair. If a post is put in the ground centrally at the back of the frame with a pulley at the top of the post, a cord can be attached to the front centre of the frame light, pass up through the pulley and have a counter-weight at the other end. When the frame light is lifted up with just two fingers, the counter-balance weight will go down and hold the light open. When work is finished the light can easily be pulled down again.

Cloches

Cloches can be difficult even on a raised bed, because when taken off a crop they have to be put somewhere, and there is rarely a space nearby (without the gardener moving) to place them. The Essex cloche is somewhat different. A framework is set down, and into this framework P.V.C. sliding panels are fitted so that crops in a raised bed can be attended to by sliding back a panel on one side of the cloche. As the cloches are made of PVC there is no glass to break.

The Garden Shed

The shed is very necessary for the keen gardener. Potting up is sometimes done in a greenhouse for it is lighter and warmer there, but even then somewhere is needed to keep the tools.

A shed is best placed with its door opposite that of the greenhouse so that plants can be transferred without the difficulty of negotiating corners. If the shed has no flooring i.e. has a concrete floor, it is quite easy to go straight in, but should there be a wooden floor on bearers a ramp may be needed. For this the Typrod ramps will be found most helpful, made originally for use at a kerbside they are usually the right height, two or more interlock to give the right width and they stack away very neatly when not in use.

If the greenhouse, shed and frame can all be incorporated on the same paved area and still leave space for free movement it will be of great advantage to the gardener.

The working bench in the shed needs to be made at a height to suit the gardener. On the wall over the bench a magnetic bar is most helpful for putting small tools such as trowel, hand fork, secateurs etc., they are easily placed on the bar, and easy to pull away. A weighted box (so that it will not move) with holes cut in it of the different sized pots is useful for keeping pots steady for the person potting with one hade hand only.

A plastic tray, as used for indoor plants to stand on, on a pulley makes a useful shelf which can be brought down to the level needed without encumbering space.

Wolf tools have a tool rack that has no spikes sticking out, but rounded smooth plastic edges. Once a gardener starts working he will soon have ideas that with help he may put into practice and will make the work easier.

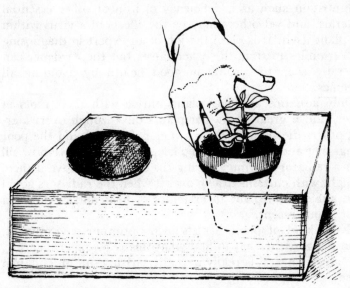

Method of keeping a pot steady when potting plants with only one hand

10 Plants in Distress

One of the disappointing things that happens in a garden is when a favourite plant becomes distressed by reason of illness or disturbance. Plant illnesses arise in several different ways.

They are often caused by fungus organisms living on the plant and these may cause the plant to wilt and die; others live on the shoots and leaves and can be easily seen in the form of white powdery mildew. Other illnesses are caused by malnutrition such as a deficiency of iron or other essential minerals, and yet others may be the effects of a virus within the plant itself. It is often the job of an expert in diagnosing such troubles to state the exact cause, but the gardener can generally keep the plants in good health by avoiding all extremes.

Only aquatics and bog plants thrive with their roots in water, and a great many pot plants die through overwatering; others die because their owner is forgetful and the poor things wilt and die of thirst. To keep a plant on a window sill over a radiator in winter during the day and to leave it there at night with curtains drawn over it when the radiators go off is to subject the plant to extremes of heat and cold which most plants resent.

Every kind of plant has its own optimum environment; often the gardener has to find what this is by experimenting, but 'green fingers' is really a quality arising out of 'common sense'.

The plant illnesses caused by fungal organisms can often

be prevented by means of fungicides though seldom cured. But most people know that 'prevention is better than cure'. This is never more true than when dealing with plants. The excellent free illustrated literature which some of the leading manufacturers of pesticides supply is well worth studying and there are also a number of good books available on the subject of plant diseases.

Plant Disturbance

There are many causes of plant disturbance, and they range from cats which are easily seen to tiny creatures such as mites which require a magnifying glass to see them in detail.

However much we may love a pet cat or dog, it is hard to forgive them when a precious plant we have nurtured and grown is scratched out of the soil or a row of expensive seed is ruined. Here again anticipation and protection is the only answer, and resort must be made to netting and evil smelling repellents. We can often allow weather conditions to assist our intelligent anticipation of other enemies. Persistent rainfall in spring and summer warns us of impending attacks of slugs and snails, and wise gardeners anxious to avoid damage to young plants put down slug pellets or granules in anticipation. Equally, prolonged hot dry weather causes greenflies and red-spider mites to breed rapidly, and the appropriate insecticide is purchased in readiness.

Spray Chemicals

There are a vast number of these available in garden centres and stores. Handicapped persons should however proceed with care in using them. It is very important that the user reads and fully understands the directions on the label. Pesticides for garden use are formulated in a variety of ways. The most usual are a) liquid concentrates for dilution in water and applying through a sprayer, b) dusts for puffing on to plants and the soil and c) aerosol liquids supplied in push-button canisters for direct application either in to the atmosphere (in a greenhouse) or directly on to plants. Probably aerosol application is most suitable for handicapped people and it is fortunate that combined insecticide and fungicide formulations are available. Combined insecticide and fungicide dust (for soil application) as well as seed dressing are also available. Never apply sprays or dusts in a strong wind; calm conditions are desirable but if a light breeze is blowing the user should be positioned on the windward side of the subject being sprayed in order to avoid spray drift or inhalation. It is advisable to wear rubber gloves.

One of the most vexing problems is that of finches pecking out the buds of flowering trees and shrubs as well as fruit trees and bushes. This usually occurs very quickly at crack of dawn, and even the cat is not on hand to prevent it happening. 'What can't be cured must be endured' must sometimes be the gardener's philosophy! Some consolation may be derived from the fact that nature generally redresses the balance and the finches which peck out the buds are also eating greenfly, the worms that throw up wormcasts on the lawn are aerating the grass roots, and even the frost which sends up the fuel bills is also breaking up the soil for us.

When pest and disease problems arise and spraying or dusting has to be done it is often a problem to know the most suitable material to purchase to give the best result. One sadly misses the friendly counter assistant in the old fashioned garden shop who was always ready with help and advice. In the modern garden centre where 'serve yourself' is the order of the day one must know just what to select to obtain the desired result. Most suppliers of pesticides issue excellent free leaflets with coloured illustrations and instructions for use of the various products available. Fortunately many of the remedies on offer bear trade names which describe their use such as 'slug pellets', 'worm killer', 'Rose fungicide' and 'moss killer' but others bear chemical names and some guidance is necessary.

BHC Used for killing certain insect pests including green fly, black fly and other coloured aphids, certain small beetles such as flea beetles, wireworms, carrot fly, and woodlice. This insecticide is available as a liquid, dust, and seed dressing. One disadvantage in using this chemical in the soil is that it is liable to cause an 'off-flavour' in root vegetables such as potatoes and carrots, but there is no possibility of this when above-ground parts are eaten as in the case of lettuces, peas and cabbages. This insecticide is also sold under the name of Lindane or Gamma-BHC.

CALOMEL DUST. Used for special purposes such as preventing club-root in cabbage family and the control of onion fly.

CHLORDANE Used for killing earthworms and ants.

DERRIS. Available in liquid and dust formulations. A non-poisonous insecticide for use against greenfly, small caterpillars and flea-beetles.

DINOCAP Available in liquid, dust and smoke formulations. For use in preventing powdery mildews.

MALATHION. An organo-phosphorus insecticide of low persistency. Kills white fly, scale insects, and raspberry beetle grubs. Has a very offensive smell.

SEVIN. Available as a dust for the control of soil pests, wasps and caterpillars.

11 Gardening in Hospitals and Day Centres

Gardening is being accepted as a therapy more and more in rehabilitation units and the occupational therapy departments of hospitals, as it can help fulfil so many purposes in helping the patients. People who have been permanently injured through a car accident, suffered a stroke, or who are badly arthritic, are helped at a rehabilitation unit to return to the ordinary routine of living as far as this is possible, and in this gardening can be helpful.

Gardening can give a wide range of exercise for the various limbs. The fingers are used in pricking out seedlings; hoeing gives arm exercise and helps hands to regain their gripping power, at the same time helping a firm stance to be maintained. A hedge cut with shears brings arm movement as well as correct co-ordination, sweeping up leaves brings a wide shoulder movement, while picking runner beans can be a bending or a stretching exercise according to where the bean pods are growing on the plants.

Understanding the correct method of doing these gardening operations is essential, otherwise the exercise is of little value, also the plants suffer. This points to the fact that if the therapist is not a gardener herself, the help of a qualified gardener is desirable to work in full co-operation with her; the patients then have the best of both worlds.

Gardening can also help in concentration and co-ordination of mind and body. If a person is hoeing between rows of plants, he or she has to concentrate so that the plants are not chopped out instead of the weeds. Gardening helps with memory; a particular skill such as taking cuttings may be demonstrated one session, and a note made as to whether the skill is remembered at a further gardening session.

When the therapist watches work being done in the garden, it gives her an opportunity to note how far a person is overcoming his difficulty and improving his abilities.

Perhaps one of the greatest values of all is when a person finds gardening can be a happy experience, opening out a new world for him, even if the hobby is only started with a few house plants. For the keen gardener who has been ill, gardening gives encouragement to get better, so that he can return to his garden and continue growing plants.

Gardening is a very wide subject, ranging from the purely technical and scientific approach to the purely aesthetic with, in between, the person who just likes to be out-of-doors and loves plants for their own sake.

For the therapist the first hurdle to cross is getting a garden started suitable for patients to work in, if one does not exist already. Usually a garden is obtained by sheer determination on the part of the therapist. With many new hospitals, areas are being set aside in the plans for a garden to be attached to the therapy department. With older hospitals, especially those in towns, sites are more difficult to come by. One London hospital has a garden in a small court bounded on three sides by very tall smoke-begrimed buildings of the hospital, on the fourth side is a one-storey building which does allow some sunlight for part of the day. This court is used to advantage, with raised beds, one ground level bed, and window boxes on the ground floor window ledges, which were fortunately just the right height for wheelchairs, so, both the patients working in the garden and those in the ward benefit from the flowers grown there.

Very often the site given for a garden is between two sets of buildings with the wind blowing between, which neither patients nor plants appreciate. Such an area needs closed fencing at one end. In these days of austerity, finances loom large. Sometimes 'Friends of the Hospital' will be able to help, particularly when they realise how valuable a garden can be to patients who are making a recovery, as well as the garden being a pleasant adjunct to the hospital grounds. At one hospital the therapist wanted to start a garden for her patients, but there were no funds available, so, on a broad tarmacadam path, she made some raised beds of tyres (see chapter 2) and also obtained an old bath from the hospital and made a raised bed of it. Once a garden is started and proved to be successful it is much easier to appeal for money to do more when it is obvious that gardening can be of real value.

The lay-out of gardens for rehabilitation and day centres will vary according to the particular needs of the patients involved, and the area available to work in.

Mention should be made of a greenhouse, which is a most valuable adjunct to patients' gardening, but it is only advisable to have one if there is time to look after it, also someone available to give attention at week-ends and bank holidays. There needs also to be someone who understands greenhouse management, such as ventilation, watering, 'damping down' in summer, and the thorough annual clean down (see chapter 9).

Plants for rehabilitation and day centres may be chosen from other chapters in this book, but there is one group to be catered for that is an exception, i.e. geriatrics. The elderly tend to think back to the plants they remember when they were young, such as wallflowers, stocks, China asters and annual candytuft. They will say a bed looks 'very nice' when planted with dimorphotheca, nemesia etc but their eyes light up when they see the 'old' flowers they are familiar with.

At day centres it creates great interest when small pieces of plants are brought from home by the individuals who attend, perhaps some herbs, a pansy or a piece of ice-plant. The bed may seem a random mixture in its planting to the outsider, but vital to the individual who is interested in how his/her plant is 'doing' each week. Quite often men are very interested in growing onions, which are an easy vegetable for a raised bed. If there are two or more men vying with one another for the best onions interest will be intense!

Appendix 1: Facilities, Tools and Books

Previous chapters have dealt with making a garden and planting with plants suitable for the gardener as well as the garden. A problem which arises for many handicapped persons is 'Who is going to do the initial work?'

In some cases a relative or friend may be able to help; if not, there are various groups of people who may possibly be contacted through the local Social Services, such as senior pupils at schools and Youth Groups. In some areas there are voluntary organisations for the 'elderly helping the elderly', for those people who have recently retired are in the main able physically. If there is a local gardening society, help may be available there.

Help is two-way: a newly-retired man may be able to help in making raised beds and the general construction of the garden, but know very little about actual gardening, while a person with a disability, such as severe arthritis, who all his life has been a gardener, can give much sound advice on plants and the growing of them.

So often help is not sought because the handicapped person does not like to ask for it, which is foolish. Once the garden is made to suit a person he or she, in most cases, can be independent.

In this chapter some notes are given as to the availability of aids and plants, all of which have been checked *at the time of writing* as being easily available, and the majority can be procured by mail order for the person who is unable to visit shops or garden centres.

There are two organisations who give help to handicapped people with information on gardening. The Disabled Living Foundation, 346 Kensington High Street, London W14 8NS. Telephone 01-602-2491

The Disabled Living Foundation is a voluntary organisation and one of its main projects is gardening. It has two demonstration gardens for disabled people and the elderly, one in Syon Park, Brentford, Middlesex and the other in Battersea Park, London.

Both gardens show a variety of raised beds and have collections of tools which may be seen and tried out by any handicapped person if a prior arrangement is made.

The Royal Horticultural Society in association with The Disabled Living Foundation has set up a similar demonstration garden in its grounds at Wisley, near Woking, Surrey, where many ways of designing a garden may be seen, and many ideas gained about selecting plants suitable for the disabled gardener.

The Disabled Living Foundation has also given advice on setting up demonstration gardens for handicapped people in public parks. Enquiries may be made at headquarters about raised beds, plants, tools etc., and leaflets on specific aspects of gardening are also published by the Foundation. Advice on planning and planting gardens is given to residential and day centres, and rehabilitation units.

The Gardens for Disabled Trust, Chairman, Mrs Kinsey, Headcorn Manor, Headcorn, Kent TN27 9NP.

The Gardens for Disabled Trust is a voluntary organisation which has two main activities; one is to raise money to give help in designing and building gardens for groups of people such as those in residential and day centres and rehabilitation units.

The other activity is running a garden club so that gardeners who have a physical difficulty may be linked together, mainly by newsletter. This newsletter not only gives advice on gardening, and answers queries where special difficulties occur, but it is also a forum where members can give their views; in this way they often help other members.

There are two volunteer instructors for the club, one in Berkshire and the other in Kent, who help members within reach. It is hoped soon to have others throughout the country.

This club also has a lending library which is valuable to members. This and other facilities are particularly helpful for the individual who lives alone, but needs some advice on gardening, and links him with other people of the same interests.

Subscription is quite small and membership is both for individuals and for groups. Further enquiries may be made to the address above.

Tools

The following is a list of aids and where they are obtainable, also nurserymen who send plants on a mail order, and a list of a small collection of books which are thought to be useful.

A list of tools giving the name and address of manufacturers and also a disability category for each tool is available from the Disabled Living Foundation, price 25p address above.

The Eclipse magnetic rack for small tools can be ordered through a hardware or tool merchant. It is manufactured by James Neill and Co (Sheffield) Ltd. Catalogue No. 947.

The Stanley knife with straight retractable blade. Knife No. 10-595 The most suitable blades are Nos. 5904 or 5905, obtainable from most hardware stores.

TyProd Ramps TyProd Ltd, Industrial Estate, Lydney, Gloucestershire.

X-panda Fencing and other types of fencing which can be sent direct from the manufacturers. Ladder and Fencing Industries (Newent) Ltd, Horsefair Lane, Newent, Gloucestershire GL18 1RP.

The Rosum Easygrow Planter: enquiries to the Gardens for Disabled Trust.

Peat Blocks for making raised bed. Alexpeat, Burnham-on-Sea, Somerset.

Essex Cloches Essex Enterprises Ltd, Robjohns Road, Chelmsford, Essex.

Watering Equipment Nethergreen Products Ltd, P.O. Box 3,

Alderley Edge, Cheshire. Mac Penny (watering equipment for indoors and out), 11-16 Marine Parade, Worthing, West Sussex BN11 3PR.

The Dolphin Agency and Advisory Service Miss G.D. Battell, 108 Ringwood Road, Walkford, Christchurch, Dorset BH23 5RF. Advice is given free by post on the best types of automation to use in your particular greenhouse, if an 11p postage stamp is sent to the above address. Details are sent on the various types of automatic heating, ventilating and watering.

Tyres for raised beds can usually be obtained free from tyre depots; a small charge may be made for lorry or coach tyres. A tyre with wheel is obtainable from a car breakers yard. A charge is made, according to size and condition of wheel.

Nurserymen who send plants on a mail order

Bressingham Gardens, Diss, Norfolk IP22 2AB. Telephone (STD) 037-988

Perennial plants, heathers, ferns, rock plants, conifers.

Reginald Kaye Ltd, Waithman Nurseries, Silverdale, Carnforth, Lancs.

Rock plants, ferns.

L.R. Russell Ltd. Richmond Nurseries, Windlesham, Surrey GU20 6LL.

Trees and shrubs.

Van Tubergen, Willowbank Wharf, Ranelagh Gardens, Fulham, London SW6 3JY.

All types of bulbs for outdoors and under glass or indoors, including the more unusual ones.

The Orphington Nurseries Ltd, Rocky Lane Gatton Park, Reigate, Surrey RH2 OTA.

Bulbs, including some of the unusual ones.

Broadleigh Gardens, Barr House, Bishops Hull, Somerset.

Specialists in small bulbs.

Burston Nurseries Ltd, North Orbital Road, St Albans, Herts.

Miniature roses.

Books

Books on gardening are very numerous indeed, and only a few have been chosen as being especially useful.

The Royal Horticultural Society, Vincent Square, London SW1P 2PE publish handbooks of which the following have been chosen, as helpful.

No.3 *Heaths and Heathers*

No.5 *Fuchsias*

No.13 *Climbing and Wall Plants*

No.14 *House Plants*

No.16 *Culinary Herbs*

No.19 *The Small Greenhouse* (the section on plants to grow is helpful)

No.24 *Bulbs Indoors*

No.25 *Plants for Shade*.

Another book published by the R.H.S. is *The Fruit Garden Displayed*, while this does deal with all types of fruit growing, there are sections dealing with rootstocks for dwarf trees, trees to choose for self-fertilisation or cross-pollination, and it also gives information on the specialised training of fruit trees.

Gardening in Window Boxes and Other Containers. by H.L.V. Fletcher, Pelham Books, 1969.

Herbs, Growing, Drying and Using. Published by Marshall Cavendish.

Indoor Gardening. A 'Ladybird Book', series 633, by J. Griffin-King. Originally intended for children, this book gives original ideas for growing plants indoors, using various things about the house. An admirable book for beginners and not costly.

Making the Best of Alpines, by Alan Bloom, available by post from Bressingham Gardens, address above. This book is excellent and has good coloured illustrations of each plant mentioned.

Adrian Bloom's Guide to Garden Plants. Jarrold Publications Book 1 Heathers; Book 2 Conifers. These are small illustrated booklets and excellent value.

Plant Propagation in Pictures, by Adrienne and Peter Oldale, published by David and Charles.

Miniature Gardens by Anne Ashbury. An interesting book giving many ideas. Also *Gardening at a Higher Level,* if still available; it might be borrowed from a library.

The Easy Path to Gardening, Reader's Digest. A well-illustrated book showing tools and various aids and methods of gardening.

Cacti and Succulents in Colour by Wim Oudshoorn, published by Lutterworth Press, 1977.

Succulents and their Cultivation by Margaret Martin and Peter R. Chapman, published by Faber and Faber, 1977.

Appendix 2: List of Tool Manufacturers

List of Manufacturers

Black and Decker, Cannon Lane, Maidenhead, Berkshire.
One-handed electric mowers.

Ceka Garden Tools, Ceka Works, Caernarvon Road, Pwllheli, N. Wales.
Florian ratchet-action pruner.

Flymo Ltd., Grey Caine Road, Bushey Mill Lane, Watford, Herts.
Flymo lawn mowers.

TH. Grace Esq., Redford House, Wiggonholt, Pulborough, Sussex. RH20 2EP.
The 'Anita Grab' for picking up rubbish.

Gravity Randall Ltd., Slinfold Horsham Sussex RH13 7RD
The Easi-Kneeler stool

Helping Hand Co., Church Road, Sandhurst, Kent.
Backsaver lifting aid.

Hozelock Ltd., Haddenham, Aylesbury, Bucks
Watering equipment for outdoors including handspray.

East Anglian Wire-Working and Engineering Co Ltd., 125 Fore Street. Ipswich IP4 1LF
The 'Gro-Thru' plant support

Stanley Tools Ltd., Woodside, Sheffield.
Junior fork or spade

H & F Whitehead, The Towers, Clayton, Bradford, Yorks BD14 6PT
The 'Bestwaye' weeder

Wilkinson Sword Ltd., Waterton Industrial Estate, Bridgend, Glamorgan CF31 3YN
Long-handled weed fork; weedfork with three foot handle; long-handled Dutch hoe and swoe
Wolf Tool Ltd., Ross-on-Wye, Herefordshire
Push pull weeder; Soil miller; terrex spade; mini-tools with rockery or three-foot light handles; handle-grip.
A. Wright and Son Ltd., 16/18 Sidney Street, Sheffield.
'Baronet' cut-and-hold flower gatherer; 'Baronet' weeder.

Index

Index

Index